Praise for

"Enlightening, inspiring, powerful, profound. Let this book light up your life!"

—Dannion Brinkley, *New York Times* best-selling author of *Saved by the Light*

"John Murphy is one of the rare individuals who see the connection between the mental, spiritual, and emotional well-being of an individual and his or her ability to direct positive energy into their business endeavors. John is a leader at shining the light on the prerequisite of a positive outlook on high end success in any work environment. I love John's books! *Zentrepreneur* will no doubt be a hit."

—Scott Stone, JD, Master Black Belt, senior director of human resources, Catalent

"If you want a strong, positive 'jump start' to your professional and personal lives, then John Murphy's books are must-reads! These books penetrate right to the core of principle-centered leadership and proactive change management. I highly recommend them to anyone looking to lead a more fulfilling life. John Murphy is a winner—and so are his books!"

—Ed Robertson, Brig. General USAF (Ret.), Communications Officer, Desert Storm

"Improvement tools and systems are not all that helpful or effective without the will to act. John Murphy's combination of positive thinking and disciplined processes is a winning approach to becoming better, no matter the business."

—Timothy D. Gill, Brig General USAF (Ret.),
process improvement Black Belt, business consultant
and Lean Six Sigma practitioner

"For the past 25 years John Murphy has contributed to Axios as a friend, mentor, consultant and director on our board. John's influence has shaped our organization's philosophy, teamwork, customer service, and culture. Ultimately, he has helped drive the type of change needed for Axios to reach the *Inc.* 500 list of fastest growing companies six times and become the 4th largest employer in our region. It now seems entirely appropriate that John is sharing with us his finest work yet, *Zentrepreneur.* This is a must read for any organization or leader planning to deliver high performance results in the hyper-competitive global economy we live in today."

—Dan Barcheski, founder and CEO, Axios Inc.

"In his exciting new book, award-winning author John Murphy demonstrates that it is the catalyst of tapping into your creative essence combined with practical hard skills that unleashes quality intuition and clarity of purpose."

—R. Michael Armstrong, Wall Street executive

"John's sage advice via *Zentrepreneur* not only hits the core issues for successful entrepreneurship, but it hits the reader too, right at the core. In simple words, John's zentrepreneur 'thinks positive, ideates well, takes risks and acts consistently,' thus converting ideas into results and dreams into monumental organizations."

—Dr. Amit Nagpal, author of *The Seven Joys of Life*, speaker, and coach, *www.dramitnagpal.com*

"John Murphy is the quintessential leader for this unique time on earth, a time in which old paradigms of success are being questioned and we must see outside the box if we intend to succeed. In *Zentrepreneur*, John helps us to recognize that each of us is, in fact, confined by 'the box' which is nothing more than our own self-imposed limitations. He then leads us out by sharing real and raw experiences of great successes and painful losses from his own life and skillfully guiding us to awaken the zentrepreneur that lies within."

—Debra Poneman, best-selling author and founder of Yes to Success Seminars, Inc.

Zentrepreneur

Get Out of the Way and Lead:
Create a Culture of Innovation and Fearlessness

By John J. Murphy

CAREER
PRESS

Pompton Plains, NJ

ZENTREPRENEUR
Cover design by Howard Grossman/12E Design
Printed in the U.S.A.

To order this title, please call toll-free 1-800-CAREER-1 (NJ and Canada: 201-848-0310) to order using VISA or MasterCard, or for further information on books from Career Press.

The Career Press, Inc.
220 West Parkway, Unit 12
Pompton Plains, NJ 07444
www.careerpress.com

Library of Congress Cataloging-in-Publication Data

CIP Data Available Upon Request.

To the zentrepreneur in you, your sacred and eternal Spirit, seeking continuous expression, exploration, and growth. Let it flow by turning your inspirations into manifestations. Namaste!

Acknowledgments

I begin every day with gratitude. There is no quicker way to transcend the ego thought system than with appreciation and thanks. Couple this with the Law of Attraction, and you bring into your life many more things to be thankful for. What better way to pray than to simply give thanks for your fingers, toes, eyesight, work, family, home, friends, and the abundance of opportunity that surrounds you? I even give thanks for my problems and challenges, quickly challenging the temptation to feel grief and interpret these outcomes as "bad." Maybe they are not! Maybe they are exactly what I need, exactly when I need them, to learn more about myself. Maybe they are gifts, blessings in disguise.

Countless people deserve thanks for this book, and I offer many examples of this throughout the book. People all over the world have offered me insights and ideas on how to apply zentrepreneurial thinking to everyday situations. I thank my parents, grandparents, children, siblings, ex-wife, clients, colleagues, students, agent, publisher, publicist, girlfriend, and the masters of the ages—all of whom have inspired me and contributed to this book in one way or another. I also thank God and the Holy Spirit for allowing me and directing me to share what I can to make this world a place of joy, peace, and freedom. I am deeply grateful.

The Sage is always on the side of virtue so everyone around him prospers. He is always on the side of truth so everything around him is fulfilled. The path of the Sage is called "The Path of Illumination."

—Tao Te Ching

Contents

Foreword

My teaching is like a finger pointing to the moon.
Do not mistake the finger for the moon.

—Buddha

When John Murphy asked me to write a foreword for *Zentrepreneur*, I was deeply honored and excited. During the past 25 years, John and I have traveled on parallel paths in our separate journeys of leading and facilitating business cultural transformations. We have both been called "Lean Sensei" or "highly respected teachers" where our roles were to work through teams and others, teaching and guiding them to bring ideas from the point of disorder to concept, and then into a place of reality delivering sustainable results. Our quests were to help change (*kai*) a place, time, a situation, a process for the better (*zen*). It was the drive for us to bring *kaizen* into reality, enabling continuous change of these ideas to make things better. I know and respect John's work in driving and leading change. His teachings provide unique insights into the "how" to make the change happen, and how to move from one point of being to another. John's work is more like a foundational instruction manual rather than just an esoteric examination into continuous improvement and excellence. Let me elaborate on this further.

Our minds are full of ideas. However, there are many occasions in our lives when these ideas of change are just stuck behind the chaos or the noise of our fears and our uncertainties. Fears and doubts prevent these ideas from becoming great results. I saw one such example when I was facilitating a learning session with a number of managers in the business practice of problem-solving. Part way through the discussions, some of these managers were unable to move from the point of chaos, doubts, and fears to a fertile place to cultivate the ideas to help them problem solve. Something was holding them back from changing for the better. After much listening and probing, I began to realize that these managers were caught in the destructive nature of doubt. They were constantly hearing the voices of "maybe not" or "says who," and it was robbing them of the resolve to move forward past the inertia. How could I help these individuals release themselves from the grips of doubt, and move them through this and into the place of ideas? I searched the bookshelves of various authors to help me gain some insights into this stage of inertia. My eyes caught the title *Beyond Doubt* by John Murphy.

Beyond Doubt provided the simple how to "let be, let go, let see, and let flow" model to move one beyond this inertia of fears, uncertainties and doubts. I read the insights, studied the techniques, and applied the knowledge. It was just like a miracle, an "a-ha" moment. The managers were able to move beyond doubt. They were able to "let be and let go" their fears and worries, "let see" the process they were trying to improve, and "let flow" the ideas to eliminate the constraints in the process. It was a roaring success. I am very sure that the many others who have applied the techniques shared in *Beyond Doubt* have experienced similar exhilarations from the Ring of Peace, after being released from the clutches and handcuffs of debilitating fears, worries, and doubts.

Now the time has come to move from *Beyond Doubt* to *Zentrepreneur*—getting the ideas from concept to reality and then onward to sustainable results. *Zentrepreneur* is the how-to guide to get us there. Each chapter walks us through a series of thought-provoking steps of what if, why, why not, who, how, when, "yeah, but," so what, and finally now what. This book will show you how to turn ideas into not just good results but great results. Let me say this, you are in for a treat. John's teachings will change the way you live and lead. As you read through each thought and word, you will be encouraged to see your confidence grow, and your ability to lead change in yourself and others will expand tremendously. You will learn through many real examples and lessons, gaining the skills that enable and empower the universal truths that serve you well to be successful.

I trust that you will enjoy and reap the benefits from reading the teachings of John Murphy, just as I do. So dig in and you will find absolutely amazing nuggets of gold that will help you make this world a better place.

—Dr. Jacob (Jake) Abraham, Lean Sensei,
former Toyota Motor Manufacturing manager

Introduction

I know of no more encouraging fact than the unquestionable ability of man to elevate his life by conscious endeavor.

—Henry David Thoreau

In 2012, I had an idea. What if I write a book about zentrepreneurship? What if I combine two powerful strategies, the art and discipline of zen practice with the science and execution of business and entrepreneurship? It was a very powerful idea, the kind of idea that keeps coming back, reminding us to pay attention. Day after day, it reappeared in my mind's eye, tapping my intuition and calling for action. It appeared in my dreams. It appeared in my work, as if I were drawing in examples and manifestations simply by giving it my attention. Rather than resist, I continued to play with the idea, contemplating its potential value. Why should I pursue this idea? I have many ideas; why does this idea deserve more attention than any other idea? What value does it add? What problems does it solve? How will it help people? How will it make the world a better place? What kind of return on investment might I get with this idea? What is the input-output correlation? I opened my mind and my heart, listening for guidance. I gave it time and attention, and nurtured it with patience, contemplation, and consideration. I shared it with members of my team and asked for honest and candid feedback. I practiced once again in my life what this book is all about.

What you are now holding in your hands is an actual example of the teachings in this book, a manifestation of a good idea. Results speak for themselves.

I have been practicing different forms of meditation, prayer, and contemplation all of my life. I begin each day with 20 to 30 minutes of application using ancient Taoist, Christian, Buddhist, Hindu, and shaman healing mantras and techniques. I do not have an either/or, right/wrong dualistic mentality when it comes to these ancient philosophies and practices. I use an "and" approach. I find the truth in all of them. To me, this is like starting the day with a mental and emotional cleansing, a shower for the soul to complement the physical shower many of us take for granted. By reducing the noise and mental chatter that tends to surround us, I feel more centered and grounded as I begin facing the challenges of the day. I "empty my bowl"—so to speak—so that I can accept "Thy Will" into my life without the subconscious denial and resistance of "my will." This is the "wisdom of emptiness" often referenced by the Dalai Lama and consistent with the teachings of Jesus, the Buddha, Lao Tzu, and many others. We all have baggage—mental, emotional, physical, social, financial, and religious. We all experience anxiety, stress, fear, and doubt. We all witness feelings of shame, guilt, grief, anger, control, and regret. We all have attachments and aversions weighing us down. To be wise and free, we have to let go to let flow.

I have also started several businesses and counseled many more. I am an entrepreneur in every sense of the word, and a consultant who travels the world learning and teaching every step of the way. In fact, the more I learn, the more I realize just how important it is to learn. Ignorance is the root cause of many problems. Put simply, we don't know what we don't know, and this ignorance causes many of the flawed assumptions and beliefs driving our perceptions and behaviors—personally and corporately. I reflect on this cause-and-effect relationship frequently, because I witness it daily. I see it with individuals ranging from well-educated executives to front-line employees. I see it with organizations ranging from global corporations with tens of thousands of employees to single-site establishments. I see it in industry after industry, country after country. This book idea would be an opportunity for me to share some of the many lessons I have learned through the years in an effort to help people and organizations overcome these self-imposed limitations. Albert Einstein once said, "The significant problems we face cannot be solved at the same level of thinking we were at when we created them."[1] To manifest great results from good ideas, we have to overcome the forces against us, many of which are hidden in the subconscious, habitual mind.

I have had many successes and I have made many mistakes. Entrepreneurs do this. So do proactive business leaders. We take risks, and challenge ourselves and our teams to explore new ground, to go where others have not yet gone before. True change agents do not allow fear and resistance to get the better of them. Innovators and pioneers are meant to explore. Uncertainty is a given. The only real challenge we face as human beings is finding and unleashing that internal pioneer, the one we all have called *Spirit*. This book aims to help us meet this challenge. Tap this extraordinary source of power and creativity, and life unfolds in miraculous ways.

Upon contemplation, research, and market assessment, the idea to write this book seemed to have value. My agent, Devra Ann Jacobs, liked it. Several of my business colleagues and associates liked it. Several of my clients liked it. My publisher liked it. So now I had to ask myself, "Why *not* write the book?" Why not go for this idea? What are the risks? What are the obstacles? Where are the constraints, including time, budget, and knowledge? What could cause this idea to fail?"

In business, we often use a tool called FMEA, or Failure Mode and Effects Analysis, to assess and mitigate risk. A simple version of FMEA requires that we brainstorm all of the potential failure modes, including the likeliness and severity of each mode, and then we come up with countermeasures to ensure success. This is no different than designing circuit breakers for a house or seatbelts for a car. The intent is to prevent or mitigate problems. In my case with this book idea, several things could go wrong: I might not finish it on time. I might not know what to say. The manuscript might not get published. People might not know about the book when it is published. People might not like it. It might not sell. The publisher and I might lose money. It could be a waste of time.

The wisdom in conducting an FMEA early in the project planning process is that it helps us avoid the "oops" syndrome later on. We anticipate possible trouble and plan ahead. We deal with the "yeah, buts" before we even hear them. This gives us more confidence in the idea and helps us prepare for the resistance that is likely to accompany it. Countermeasures for this book idea include:

- Draw from 30 years of personal experience and market research with global businesses to make the book practical and interesting. Use real examples and stories.

- Develop an effective project plan to meet the publishing deadline. Set a realistic target.

- Use my platform of other critically acclaimed and award-winning books to market this book, including speeches, workshops, distribution networks, and media events.

- Establish a marketing plan and budget.

- Contract a professional publicist with a positive track record.

- Get endorsements from credible people in a variety of roles and settings.

Good ideas are not without risk. Eventually, there comes a time to step up and take a swing. As Wayne Gretzky once said, "We miss 100 percent of the shots we never take." Good ideas will never manifest into great results if we do not act on them. I chose to act on this book idea. In fact, I have elected to act on countless ideas in my life—some good, some questionable. Each of the chapters in this book will give you a look into a few of these ideas, including many that might not seem like good ideas at the start. Often, what appear to be mistakes or painful losses are really blessings in disguise. I will share the good, the bad, and the ugly, all with the intent to offer practical experience, wise counsel, and humble guidance.

Use the questions, methods, and practices in this book to stimulate creative thinking, positive ideas, and great results. Share it with team members and employees to help them see outside the box. Keep in mind that most people do not even recognize the box they are in. We don't know what we don't know. Ignorance is the root cause of virtually all of our problems, as well as the fear and resistance we witness every day. Uncertainty breeds doubt in the unenlightened mind and limits our resolve. Overcome these self-imposed barriers and you awaken the zentrepreneur in you. It is alive and well, and eagerly awaiting your call. Listen for it, look for it, and then act on it. Give yourself the freedom you deserve. The key is in your mind.

1

What If?

Imagination is everything.
It is the preview of life's coming attractions.

—Albert Einstein

In 1988, I got fired. The new owners of the company I was working for decided they no longer needed me after an acquisition in 1986. It was a mutual agreement. I had essentially eliminated my job. It was time to move on. The timing wasn't all that great. I had very little savings, and my wife was pregnant with our second child. I remember thinking to myself, "What should I do now? What direction do I go in?" Then I had an idea. What if I start a consulting company? What if I transition from my former job as a corporate executive to a small business owner? What would that be like? What value might that add? Why do it? Why not do it? What are the risks? What are the rewards? Who might be able to help me? How would I do it? When would I do it? Where are the constraints? What could I learn from the experience? What could I contribute to the world by doing so? How does this idea feel to me? Is it something I dream about? Do I feel passion? The questions went on and on.

If I have learned anything over the many years I now have invested in business management and consulting, it is that there is no scarcity of ideas. We are surrounded by creativity, enthusiasm, expansion, and growth. All we have to do is look for them. It is human nature, fueled by our spiritual nature. We are meant to grow—physically, mentally, emotionally, and spiritually. There is really no stopping this. It is the way of the world. It is the *Tao*, the "great current" of life. Resistance to what is natural is a fast and easy way to experience stress, exhaustion, anxiety, and accelerated physical aging.

I believe there is a zentrepreneur in all of us. We all have ideas, and we all like to see them manifest into something positive. So what holds us back? Is it that no one asks us for our ideas? Is it that we choose not to share them? Is it that people do not listen to us when we do share them? What is it? Why is it that so many ideas remain just that: ideas. How can business leaders break through these limiting barriers to tap the creative power of their teams? Think about how many ideas might be lost in your organization because there is no easy and effective way to channel them into action.

One of the methods I use to capture good ideas and turn them into great results is called *kaizen*. This is a Japanese word that comes from two words, *kai* and *zen*, which essentially translate into "good change." We use kaizen events to accelerate good change. Typically, these events last about three to five days with a mission of making change during the event, not planning it for some other time. A team is generally commissioned and trained a few weeks ahead of time, and preliminary data is then collected, mapped, and displayed. During the event, the targeted process is analyzed, and improvement ideas are identified, tested, and implemented. These are positive, proactive, high energy, or *zenergy*, events with great results as the norm. It is a very practical, efficient, and effective method for applying zentreprenuership and positive change in any culture. Kaizen events are significantly different from traditional meetings where people sit around and talk about changes without anything actually getting done. They are an immediate demonstration of culture change.

After facilitating hundreds of kaizen events over the years, one thing has become clear: no two events are exactly alike. Every event has variables, including the participants, need, scope, circumstances, data, constraints, resistance, energy levels, leadership capability, support, and dozens of other factors. Therefore, we have to learn to play with the hand we are dealt to get the results we desire. The key to running a successful event is to clarify the team mission, purpose, and expectations. From there, we have to listen, empathize, and trust one another.

Some of the easiest kaizen events to understand and run involve workplace organization. In other words, consider how much time can be wasted searching for things if they are not exactly where we want them and not ready for use when we need them. This can apply to a maintenance shop, an operating room, a kitchen, a laboratory, an office, a laptop, a closet, or any other environment. Now imagine a surgeon searching for a clean scalpel or a pit crew looking for a wrench while people are waiting and in need. Not being ready is not being productive.

In a typical kaizen event aiming at workplace organization, we begin by defining and measuring the current state. How are things done now? How are we organized? What do we really need? How are we using what we need? Map the process and populate the map with undisputable facts and data. Record the process on video if it will help clarify things. Follow operators through the process to see how they do whatever it is they do. If they are cooks in a restaurant, how do they go about preparing meals? If they are maintenance technicians, how do they go about servicing the equipment? Where is time being wasted? What are the inefficient activities or sequences? Establish a baseline of measures and frustrations.

The kaizen team usually spends three to four weeks prior to the event collecting this data and preparing to display it in a meaningful, impactful way. We then begin the three- to five-day kaizen event by using this data to align all team members and the leadership team with a clear summary of the current state. Normally, this provokes some very interesting dialogue between the baseline team and the leadership team who comes in each day for a 30- to 60-minute briefing. Do we really do it that way? Does it really take that long? Do we really have that much re-work?

Once we have consensus on the current state, we analyze why things are the way they are. Why do we do it that way? Why do we take that long? Why do we have that much re-work? This analysis leads us to the root causes, the level at which we want to solve the problem. This is how we sustain the improvements. If we truly get to the root cause, the symptoms should go away and not come back. In a workplace organization kaizen event, the root causes are often related to flawed assumptions leading to flawed policy, procedure, process design, and organization. To correct this, we might have to rearrange the work flow, relocate the material and equipment, and change certain policies and procedures. If we were doing this in your kitchen, laundry room, or tool shop, where are the best places to locate the tools you need to do the job in the most productive, user-friendly manner?

When teams get together to evaluate a current state situation that is wasteful and frustrating, it is exciting to see how they open up to change. Kaizen events are not something we do *to* people. We do them *with* people. We involve the users of the process, listening to them and asking for their input and experiences. We guide them through the analysis and collectively search for better alternatives. We tap their creativity and innovate together, trying the ideas, and testing them for risks and results. And when we have found a better way—quickly—we adopt it and institutionalize the new change as evidence that we walk our talk. We draft the new policy or procedure, and we get it signed in the event, not weeks later. We train everyone on the new way, and monitor it for effectiveness. We follow up with additional kaizen events to make the process even better. These kaizen events are all done in the spirit of continuous improvement, so we are never really finished. We just continue to make things better and better as new ideas surface and opportunities present themselves.

One example of this zenergy comes from a kaizen event with a client in Canada in 2010. The executive sponsor of the project opened the event with a few words to clarify expectations, offer support, and reiterate a sense of urgency. He was setting the tone for action. He was looking for a way to proactively collect some good ideas and quickly turn them into great results. This was a project aiming to correct a dysfunctional master planning and scheduling system, resulting in unacceptable customer service levels, poor use of assets, and millions of dollars in backorders and lost sales. My role was to provide real-time training, guidance, and kaizen facilitation.

Following the executive sponsor's comments, the project leader asked the team how we would handle any differences of opinion that prevented us from reaching consensus on designing and implementing a better way. This project leader also happened to be the manager in charge of the planning and scheduling departments. Clearly, he wanted the last say in any matter of dispute. This was "his baby" and he was a bit defensive because the data suggested it was quite "ugly." The team responded to his question by kicking around several ideas ranging from voting to autocracy. It seemed obvious to me that the team was already demonstrating some fear, insecurity, and distrust in the consensus decision-making process. I could only smile. This is quite common at the start of most kaizen events. The average team gets nervous.

After a few minutes of struggle with this question, the executive sponsor caught my smile and suggested that I might have something to say. All eyes turned toward me, and the room became quiet. I allowed the silence to sink in for a moment, and then I simply asked if we had any *geniuses* on the team. At first, a few people snickered,

perhaps thinking I was kidding. Then there was an awkward silence. So, I repeated my question, "Seriously, do
we have any geniuses on the team?" I scanned the faces
around the large conference table, finally pausing at the
team leader. No one said a word. At that point, I suggested that because we had no geniuses *on* the team, we agree
to go with the genius *of* the team, a disciplined process
that I would facilitate. I also challenged the team to remember that I said this because by the end of day two, we
would return to the subject to see if we were fully aligned
and in true consensus. This challenge meant we had to
pull together quickly and put aside our personal agendas.
It also put pressure on me to do my job.

Whenever we see high-performance teams "in flow,"
we witness grace, harmony, and power in action, the
yin and yang of the Tao. We see what is referred to in
Taoism as *wu wei*, or effortless manifestation. We observe
genuine alignment, pure harmony, and authentic synergy. Personal agendas take a back seat, and the fearful ego
thought system is transcended to a new, heightened sense
of awareness and realization. We are all one! We are all in
this together. The all too common "me-opic" perspective
("What's in it for me?") is replaced with "we-opic" vision
and intent ("What's in it for we?"). The power of unity reveals itself to us and we feel awakened, alive, and empowered. We experience a connectedness to one another, a
collective mind and a heightened sense of consciousness.

We gain courage, openness, empathy, compassion, and intuitive guidance. Worries and stresses melt away. Fear and doubts dissolve. Ideas flow and creativity expands. Time seems to stand still. Think of this like a symphony orchestra made up of many diverse functional areas now all playing as one. There is pure harmony. The zenergy and synergy are extraordinary.

Of course, to experience this kind of flow of power and grace, there are many barriers to overcome and limiting beliefs to release. We cannot tap this infinite field of possibilities if we are afraid or in a state of apathy, denial, or resistance. We have to detach from the habitual, autopilot mind and think outside our mental boxes. We have to delete the negative programs and limiting memes of the mind. We have to empty our bowl. We have to open our receptors. We have to let go to let flow.

Zenergy is ineffable. It is difficult to describe with words. Like the words grace, love, joy, forgiveness, and compassion, it must be experienced to be understood. People describe it in different ways, but the only way to know zenergy is to feel zenergy. Think of it as a divine energy field, a cosmic soup surrounding, connecting, and penetrating us. It is within us and we are within it. It is sacred intent. It is life force. It is Source energy. To tap zenergy, we must lead from the heart and soul, fearlessly and without doubt. The intellect, while critically important to effective leadership, will not show us—or anyone else—true Spirit. We must go deeper, to the level where people "get the chills."

Zenergy is fluid and dynamic, with no beginning and no end. It is always present, a frequency or vibration that plays continuously—even if we are not tuned into it. Think of it like soulful music playing on a continuous radio station. It is present whether we are listening to it or not. It is constant and effortless in its manifestation. We are not inspired and creative by trying to be inspired and creative. Rather, we are inspired and creative when we let go of our resistance and align with the higher vibration of zenergy, inspiration, and creativity. This is our core spiritual essence, beneath and beyond the ego thought system that we are conditioned with from birth.

The ego thought system is a universal, fear-based way of thinking that is dualistic, comparative, competitive, and divisive. It is common for human beings to buy into this thought system, something we often refer to as someone's "ego." The ego thought system thinks the same way no matter who thinks it. It is not that we have a personal ego; rather, we have a connection to one, universal way of thinking that denies us of understanding our true, authentic, Spiritual self. The ego thought system gives us a false identity and feeds us with fear and an addiction to drama. It takes courage and wisdom to let go of this way of thinking and see the world differently.

To access our spiritual essence, we must release ego thinking—disempowering thoughts such as apathy, greed, selfishness, pride, anger, guilt, insecurity, and fear. There is no pretending to be in Spirit, as it requires honesty and integrity to flow. One cannot pretend to be honest. One cannot fake integrity. One cannot fool universal grace. When we witness zenergy, it is not unusual to feel a sense of awe, a sense of reverence, perhaps even physical vibration and tingles. This is a connection with Spirit, a moment of inspiration and revelation. Sage leaders and zentrepreneurs understand that by being "in Spirit," we connect with the Spirit in others. This is a soul-to-soul relationship, a link that transcends time and space. It is infinite, omnipotent, and omnipresent. It is what brings out the best in all of us, inspires us, and truly defines us as authentic leaders.

People in leadership positions all over the world frequently comment to me on how challenging it is to sustain change and lead true, genuine cultural transformations. "People resist change," they tell me, disclosing a flawed and very disempowering assumption and excuse. The zentrepreneur disagrees. People are actually designed for change—physically, emotionally, socially, and mentally. As Heraclitus once said, "Nothing endures but change."[1]

As human beings, we are in a constant state of change. Our bodies replenish the 50-trillion-plus cells within us about every four years. We change our minds, clothes, diets, and lifestyles. We sleep, awaken, grow, adapt, learn, expand, age, laugh, and cry. We are continuously changing at the physical, mental, and emotional levels as we make our way through life. These changes are natural and effortless. They just happen. Thoughts come and go organically. Hunger, aches, feelings, moods, temptations— all these come and go. This is human and natural. Life force is effortless. A tree does not have to try to grow; a rose does not have to work hard to blossom. They are meant to grow and blossom.

At a spiritual level, all of life is in perfect harmony and balance, beyond most human awareness, perception, and comprehension. This is divine power and grace, the perfect yin-yang nature of the universe. When we know, experience, and appreciate authentic power and grace, we allow ourselves to be more effective leaders, because we are aligning with a much greater source of knowledge than our limited, independent minds. Our very presence brings light and energy to people in darkness and doubt. We use contrast to our advantage. We see the context of the content, the big picture. We become a breath of fresh air, a symbol of hope, optimism, and positive energy. With zenergy and grace, all things seem possible. Miracles become the norm, because we see them happening all the time. We are living the miracles.

To lead with zenergy, we must first experience it. We must know it from the heart, not the head. We must feel it and channel it with the heart, for it is with the heart that we communicate with Spirit. This is a challenge for many head-strong, analytical leaders. Zenergy is an emotional intelligence, not an intellectual, abstract debate. It requires a sense of surrender to a higher power, a transcendence of the ego thought system. To lead with zenergy, we must recognize and admit that we do not have all the answers. In fact, we must acknowledge that we know very little with absolute certainty. Sure, we have all kinds of facts and data. We are loaded with historical information and conditioning. But in truth, we know very little. True knowledge is about certainty and predictability. At the human level, very little is certain. Life can change in a split second, far beyond our control. It is only the ignorant, insecure, and arrogant ego that thinks differently. It is the ego that denies and repels zenergy, keeping people in the dark. How often do we confuse knowing something with *thinking* we know something? How many years passed with people thinking the world was flat? Who would have guessed that we are hurling through space at more than 65,000 miles per hour, on a sphere spinning at more than 1,000 miles per hour? The eye and the mind can be deceiving. To truly know something, we must be it. Even then, we might know very little at all.

Earlier in this chapter, I mentioned that I would challenge the kaizen team to see if we were in true consensus by the end of the second day of the five-day event. Day one was going reasonably well, but we were not yet experiencing the "genius of the team." We were making progress on getting aligned with current-state facts and data, an early step in cultivating a collective mind. But there was still a great deal of fear and doubt among the team. How do I know this? I felt it. I paid attention to it. The zenergy was low. People were sitting around the conference table, complaining and rationalizing, attacking and defending. The team was caught in an "ego battle." Keep in mind, the ego thought system thrives on separation, comparison, drama, pride, and competition. When people tap into and accept this very human thought system, these battles will often take place without anyone even aware of it. For me, this is like watching a movie or a film, and thinking it is real. The villain and the hero play out their roles, tantalizing the audience with the yin and yang of Hollywood productions, and then the cast members celebrate opening night together as one team. We all play roles in life, and we frequently get caught up in conflict, but this does not define who we are. We are not what we do. At the human level, we are beings, not doings.

To reenergize the kaizen team and cultivate a state of flow, I introduced a cause and effect tool called a Causal Circle. This tool challenges a team to find key drivers and "leverage points" that could lead to quick and dramatic changes. This exercise got people on their feet, applying systems thinking to a systems problem—in other words, they examined the entire system rather than individual components. This is a key point. When people try to solve a systems problem with independent solutions, they will no doubt experience "side effects," sometimes making the situation even worse. This is like taking a drug for one symptom and causing several others. Systems problems (i.e., interdependent, integrated processes) require systems solutions, making it absolutely key to find the right leverage points. In other words, a relatively simple change at a point of leverage can lead to profound and sustainable benefits across the whole system.

Causal Circle

The Causal Circle is a tool that allows the user to evaluate the cause and effect relationship between multiple UDEs, or Undesirable Effects. It is important to note that some UDEs can be major drivers or causes to other UDEs. Look for these relationships by evaluating the number of arrows going out from each UDE. How many other UDEs does it cause, if any? Also look for what is causing this UDE. Search for the "lever" that, if changed, could reduce or eliminate multiple UDEs. Make sure the UDEs are factual and measurable. Find the "vicious circles" where two to three UDEs cause each other.

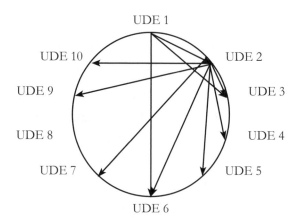

Exercise: Using the list of UDEs, complete the circle and identify one to two critical leverage points. From a systems perspective, what is causing most of the problem? What needs to change?

UDE 1: Too many interruptions during the day.

UDE 2: We/I do not have enough time to do what is most important.

UDE 3: We/I feel stressed a lot.

UDE 4: Our/My problems keep repeating themselves.

UDE 5: Our/My direction is not clear.

UDE 6: The people we/I need to help are often not available.

UDE 7: We have too many fires to put out.

UDE 8: Our costs are too high.

UDE 9: Our Right First Time (RFT) quality is low.

UDE 10: We are not making enough money.

The team worked throughout the afternoon, learning to challenge the system, not one another. Before long, personal agendas were set aside, and a collective mind was beginning to take root. The results from the Causal Circle were quite revealing, leading the team to discover four critical leverage points, without disagreement. These were indisputable drivers causing multiple undesirable effects. In addition, I had the team post any and all fears or doubts they were experiencing about the current system, the potential changes, and the expectations of the kaizen event itself. This too was revealing, as it helped me understand the skepticism and anxiety that was blocking zenergy and obstructing authentic team empowerment. By admitting, discussing, and releasing these fears, we were now in a state of mind that enabled creativity and genuine innovation. Day two then came together with enthusiasm, power, and zenergy—the perfect combination to uncover creative alternatives and win-win solutions. The result? By the end of day two, the team leader and the entire team expressed no doubt whatsoever that we were in consensus on the current state, the key leverage points, and several preliminary ideas on how to solve the problem at the root cause level. The zenergy in the room was increasing and the "lights" were coming on. The team members and the collective team were beginning to get into a state of flow. With three days to go, we were now ready to detail the changes we wanted to make, prepare a plan, and get the ideas implemented quickly. We also reached consensus with the executive team at the end of the week on several key policy changes that had to be made at the senior management level, a form of discipline being proposed up, and a reflection of the cultural transformation taking place. We were leading up! These senior management policy changes were unexpected but accepted, because they were credible, rational, and convincing, representing a significant shift in the traditional top-down management paradigm. This is a typical result for applying the art and science of zentrepreneurship. We awakened the genius of teamwork through proactive involvement and a focused kaizen event.

I feel blessed to have participated in kaizen events all over the world. Time and time again, I see people open up and share a plethora of good ideas. These ideas are then organized, tested, and applied immediately. There is no suggestion box. There are no contests. There are no bonuses for good ideas. At best, the team might get lunch provided or a nice certificate of recognition. Nonetheless, motivation rises. People start getting excited. Problems are addressed quickly and effectively. Low-hanging fruit is picked now, not later when things begin to spoil. Higher challenges are addressed during the events with executive briefings, so that the authority needed to make these changes is granted. Action is taken and momentum builds.

To accomplish great results quickly, the leader must be centered, energized, poised, and committed. High-performance teamwork is inspired by leaders who step up and demonstrate heartfelt passion, conviction, and determination, not doubt. As Gandhi put it, we must be the change we want to see in the world. We must lead by fearless example and demonstrate the innovative behaviors we want to see in others. We all have the capacity to be creative. We all have the potential to tap into zenergy and experience flow. Stop and ask yourself how you get centered at the beginning of each day. Do you start your day with anxiety and stress, fueled by the morning news or an endless "to do" list? Or do you allow yourself time each morning for an internal shower, through quiet meditation and contemplation? Many people would not consider starting the day without a physical shower. We wake up and allow time for this common habit. Do we allow the same time for a mental and emotional cleanse? I know I do. I commit at least 20 to 30 minutes every morning for meditation and contemplation. I choose to start my day in peace—not panic or paranoia.

Meditation is simply the practice of quieting the mind and letting go. It is about getting mental and emotional chatter out of the way. It is more about listening than asking or analyzing. It allows us to hear our own heart beat and synchronize it with our breathing. It allows us to elevate our energetic vibration, frequency, heart coherence, and consciousness. It allows us to soothe our vital organs and release dangerous toxic energy by using healing sounds and mantras, like "ahhhhhh" for the heart and "shhhhhhh" for the liver. Try this by taking a deep breath, focusing on the health and well-being of the vital organ in mind and then releasing the healing sound or mantra. *Mantra* simply means instrument of the mind. It is a tool that can be used to focus attention and deliver results. With the ahhhhhh sound, you should feel a calming vibration in your heart. With the shhhhhh mantra, you feel a mild expansion of the liver, like it is a filter being cleansed. Is it any coincidence that we often say shhhhhh when we want someone to calm down or be quiet? The liver is a vital organ for health and well-being. If it is not in balance, our moods range from deep depression to being "livid" and angry. There are many different forms of meditation, several of which I use, but any method that works for you is invaluable. All you have to do is find a technique you like and practice it.

The same is true for contemplation. This is the practice of suspending analysis, criticism, and judgment. It releases us from divisive, dualistic ego thinking and broadens our perspective. The mystic Rumi once wrote, "There is field beyond right and wrong. I will meet you there."[2] This non-dualistic comment reveals the essence of contemplation. It reminds us to put judgment aside and open our minds to the bigger picture of healthy contrast. Use these techniques to find and enable your emotional center throughout the day: Stop and consider multiple points of view. Invite pushback. Seek to understand. Let go of any emotional baggage weighing you down. The people you lead will notice the difference.

One of the most fundamental keys to running successful kaizen events or any other creative problem-solving exercise is asking the question "What if?" What if we try this? What if we change that? What if we organize things differently? What if we stop doing some of the wasteful things we are doing? These are questions of playful possibility, not criticism and judgment. The open mind is contemplative. The closed mind is skeptical, analytical, and critical. There is a time for sowing and a time for reaping. Know the difference. Nothing kills a good idea quicker than a closed mind. IBM passed on the idea

of Microsoft. Kodak passed on the idea of Xerox. The
first Apple computer was made out of wood. The idea
of Federal Express was considered a joke. Sam Walton,
founder of Wal-Mart, was not taken seriously on Wall
Street. Amazon lost money for years before it got traction.
Have you seen photos of the Wright brothers trying to get
the first plane off the ground? And how was the quality of
those first cameras? The list goes on and on.

Everything we see around us started with an idea. The
cars we drive, the phones we use, the buildings we live or
work in all began in the mind's eye. Someone somewhere
dreamed about and imagined the possibility of such a
manifestation. Someone boldly asked, "What if?" Now
we have it. The creative mind works best when it is free of
anxiety and stress. Children are often playful and imagi-
native because they do not carry a lot of chatter in their
minds. Adults can struggle with this, especially at work or
in an environment where we are bombarded with negative energy and judgment. When we feel free and at ease,
we intuit more easily. We solve problems more effectively.
We think more clearly and creatively. When we let go of
the resistance, we let flow with zenergy.

I began this chapter by offering a very important
"what if" for me in 1988. What if I start a consulting company? What if I take a chance and start a business from
scratch? What would that be like? As of this writing, my

company is celebrating its 25th birthday! Hmmm... Good idea? I believe so!

Checklist for Success

- I allow myself quiet time every morning to get centered and in Spirit.

- I allow myself time throughout each day to contemplate and play with ideas.

- I suspend judgment and disbelief when brainstorming.

- I believe I am a creative being contributing to the results I experience in life.

- I believe all people are creative beings with the capacity to manifest dreams.

- I look for value in every idea and person I meet.

- I see opportunities where others see problems.

- I look for systems solutions to systems problems.

- I use effective tools to identify root causes and solve problems rationally.

- I ask "What if?" A lot!

2

Why?

*Things which matter most must never be at
the mercy of things which matter least.*

—Johann Wolfgang Von Goethe

In 2012, I offered an idea to a major client of mine. I suggested they use a proven process called *baseline analysis* to assess the overall health and stability of the organization. This process is like going to a capable and competent team of doctors for a thorough examination of your critical operating systems. The baseline analysis process accomplishes several things:

- It grounds the leadership team in reality using brutal facts and data.

- It determines major root causes and leverage points to systems problems.

- It identifies and charters five to six high-priority, strategic projects.

- It establishes a baseline for measurement of progress and accountability.

- It focuses and aligns the leadership team with systems thinking.

In other words, a highly competent team of experts gives the organization a comprehensive examination with the intention of making significant step changes. Why is this important? Nothing saps zenergy quicker than putting a lot of time and effort into activity and projects that do not really matter. People get frustrated, results suffer, fingers get pointed, and tension and stress compound. Content without context is meaningless, so it absolutely necessary to examine the entire system.

A baseline analysis begins with a capable, competent, cross-functional team trained in meaningful data collection and analysis. The data collected and analyzed include customer and market information, competitor information, operational information, organizational information, support systems information, and financial information. In the case of this client, we assembled a team of approximately 15 subject matter experts across the business, trained them on the baseline analysis process and tools, and then evaluated two major "value streams" (products flowing from start to finish representing "the way work is done around here"). This analysis took about one month and the findings were astonishing for most of the people involved, including the executives briefed throughout the process. This company, a very large one in its industry, was wasting more than $50 million per year with no solutions in place to correct the overall systems problems. In fact, very few people were even aware of the problems.

You might ask how this is possible. How can so much waste and inefficiency be hidden? How can people not know? Did this company not have a scorecard? Yes it did, but it was missing some very critical measures, such as inventory turns and value-stream cycle time. In other words, it did not measure the *flow* of that which the customer was paying for. Some of the metrics actually disrupted flow and incented the wrong behaviors, like buying too much material all at once. Other metrics revealed symptoms, but did nothing to address the root causes. Did this company not have projects underway? Yes indeed, it did. Everyone appeared busy with little time to spare. There was no shortage of activity. However, activity was being confused with productivity. There is a significant difference. Did this company not have capable and committed people? Yes it did. The people in this company are wonderful, talented, caring human beings. Were these projects and assignments not relevant? This is the multi-million-dollar question. Some projects were relevant and some were not. Some even risked making things worse from an overall systems perspective. Did this company not have projects prioritized and underway that would address the key leverage points costing the company fortunes? The brutal answer to this question is no. A high-level, fact-based, data-driven value stream analysis had never been done. Managers simply picked projects that addressed symptoms, not root causes. The emphasis was on correction, not prevention. The management team was spending more time being reactive than proactive. Lagging indicators were taking priority over leading indicators.

Stop and ask yourself: How do I identify and prioritize improvement projects? What methods do I use? What data do I collect? How do I collect it? Who collects it and how do I turn the data into meaningful information and intelligence? How do the projects I select optimize the overall system and not just a single point (department or function) within the system? How do I evaluate the win-win effect of the projects and avoid costly side effects? How do I use the project selection process to focus, educate, mobilize, and motivate the people who have to carry out the execution? How do I use the data and analysis to align and inspire the leadership team? How do I ensure that the people leading the organization are grounded in facts and the day-to-day reality of creating value? Opinions based on unchallenged assumptions can be very costly. Ultimately, ignorance and assumption are the root causes of most of our problems.

Chances are your company has plenty of opportunity to improve, to turn good ideas into great results. The real challenge is not in finding enough ideas or projects; it is in limiting the number of projects to a critical few that really matter. One really great project can outweigh 100 insignificant ones. Too many projects and ideas scattered randomly throughout the organization may lead to some improvement, but rarely do they lead to true step change. The real potential is in the gaps and in the relationships between the functions, where no one is looking. Find one long-enough lever, and you can move the world.

The baseline analysis we did in 2012 was a major turning point for this client. It is not uncommon to hear many members of the leadership team say, "We didn't know what we didn't know. We were walking in the dark." The comprehensive baseline analysis process revealed significant opportunity for this client with just five projects. These projects tied the whole site together, "connecting the dots," as the site leader likes to say. The difference is that these five projects were not single department projects. They were bold "systems" projects requiring cross-functional participation from multiple sites, levels, competencies, and disciplines. Six months later, the client was experiencing profound cultural transformation, and one project alone paid for all of the consulting, resourcing, and training for years.

W. Edwards Deming, the grandfather of Total Quality Management, once said, "Put a good person in a bad system and the bad system wins, no contest."[1] He also said, "Hard work and best efforts without the guidance of profound knowledge may well be the root of our ruination."[2] His words could not ring more true to dozens of experiences I have had with organizations around the world. I have trained thousands of people on leading change, and I have facilitated countless baseline analysis events to identify the best place to start. In virtually all cases, I find good people in very frustrating, misaligned, dysfunctional systems. I consistently find good ideas lost in the turmoil and invaluable human potential lost in space.

The question "why?" simply reminds us to exercise our right brain, our intuition, and contextual understanding. Why do I do what I do? Why does it really matter? What value does it add? How does it impact the customer and the bottom line? If I do more of it, will the organization reap more benefit? Will the customer want more of it? Will the customer pay more for it? Will people appreciate it more? Will it make things safer or more environmentally friendly? Will it improve flow, or is it just another form of waste, disguised as activity and busy work? How relevant is what I do? What difference will the project or idea really make? How will I know? What metrics or key performance indicators (KPIs) will it impact? What do the data say? What evidence do I have that the idea or project is relevant?

Achieving and sustaining true high-performance teamwork and results requires working backward to some extent. We start with an end in mind and move upstream from there. What is the vision or response I intend to realize? What are the results expected? What is the voice of customer (VOC) really telling us? What is the value we intend to deliver? What is the value proposition we offer? What is the goal, stated in a clear, compelling, articulate way? Do we all see it as a team? Are we connecting the dots? Is the story clear? Is the mission clear? Are we aligned? How can we truly be aligned if the end in mind is not clear? Do we see as one, or are we confused about priorities and expectations? Great results require great teamwork, and great teamwork requires shared vision and understanding.

We can also use the question "why?" to uncover root causes, gain deeper understanding, and identify potential opportunities. For example, whenever we have a problem, we can play with it a bit by asking why. A contemplative, root cause analysis tool now made famous worldwide by Toyota is referred to as the "5 Whys." It is suggested that by asking why approximately five times (meaning five levels deep), we can identify meaningful, transformational change opportunities. I like to give this simple example in my workshops. Let's say George was late for work—an undesirable effect. Why was George late? One level why: because his car would not start. Why did his car not start? Second level why: because his battery was dead. At this level, we could either blame George or the battery. Third level why: why was the battery dead? George left the lights on. Why did George leave the lights on? He forgot. Why did he forget? He is human. People make mistakes. We all know this. We see it every day. Now, what can we do to solve the problem at this level from a systems perspective?

The 5 Whys

UDE: George was late!

1st Level	His car would not start	or No alternative plan
2nd Level	The battery was dead	or Did not plan ahead
3rd Level	The lights were left on	or Did not anticipate problem
4th Level	Forgot to turn them off	or Did not do an FMEA
5th Level	No reminder or help	or Did not know how

Note: It often takes five levels of why to get to the true root cause. It is at this level that we solve problems in a sustainable way.

The "5 Whys" questioning technique is what often leads to what is known in Japan as *poka-yoke*, or mistake-proofing. It stimulates thinking around how we can design "systems-solutions" to avoid common errors. In this case, it leads to innovations like signals to remind George—and the rest of us—to turn our lights off. In some cases, the car will turn the lights off automatically for us. Innovations like these do not come from surface-level thinking. As Einstein once put it, "The significant problems we face cannot be solved at the same level of thinking we were at when we created them." We have to get outside the box to even see the box entrapping us. We can start this process by simply asking and contemplating "why?"

The effective change agent uses intuition, contemplation, and discernment to choose ideas and actions wisely. The question "why?" helps us exercise this thinking process and develop these skills. It also helps us uncover critical success factors to sell our ideas and get them to work. If we can't sell the idea, we can't turn it into great results, because we need help, teamwork, and support. Change is often met with skepticism and resistance; many people would rather accept the status quo and play it safe. The zentrepreneur seeks to build a constituency for change, a team of committed people who are eager to help turn vision into reality.

To build a constituency for change, the zentrepreneur builds on these characteristics:

- Credibility.

- Courage.

- Belief.

- Ownership.

- Responsibility.

- Accountability.

- Intuition.

- Initiative.

- Perseverance.

- Optimism.

A good idea without credibility and salesmanship is going nowhere. People must see the value in the idea and believe in it. If an entrepreneur cannot convince a bank or investment group to support an idea with money, it may never get off the ground. The same is true for the zentrepreneur. If you cannot convince your boss, colleagues, or potential team members that your "good idea" is worthy of their support, you will not spark the zenergy to see it through to great results. It doesn't matter if it is a good book idea, a good process improvement idea, a good product development idea, or a good new business idea. No credibility, no commitment. No commitment, no zenergy!

The real secret to gaining credibility is in doing your homework and knowing your audience. Start by getting the facts. What is the basis for your idea? What is the problem it will solve or the need it will fill? What is the evidence of the problem or need? How big is it? How often does it happen? How do you know? Quantify it. Is this fact or assumption? What kind of resistance are you likely to encounter? Why will people push back? What is in it for them? How do you know? Think carefully about the perception people have of you and your ideas. Do they trust that you know what you are doing and talking about? What is the basis for this trust? What does your track record reveal? What are your credentials? Use the following tool, called Force Field Analysis, to list the forces for and against you and your idea. This will help build credibility.

Forces for the idea	Forces against	Countermeasures
⟶	⟵	? ? ?
Why do it? What is the value?	Why not do it? What are the obstacles?	Plan accordingly. how will you overcome?

Fear is a very powerful barrier to success, and it takes courage to confront it. In fact, fear is where many good ideas first get lost. We have a good idea or an inspiration—a zen moment—but we talk ourselves out of it. We are afraid to speak up or share the idea. We are afraid of rejection. We fear criticism and judgment. We worry about making mistakes. We resist failure, and in doing so we resist success. These outcomes are two sides to the same coin.

I have had thousands of my ideas rejected throughout the years. This comes with the territory as a writer, speaker, entrepreneur, change agent, and consultant. I am in the business of leading transformational change, a business often met with resistance. If I listened to and accepted every rejection I have experienced, I would be nowhere. The key for me has been in listening to the reasons why I was being rejected and going back to do my homework. The best place to start looking when you are rejected is the mirror. What do I need to change in the way

I am pitching the idea? What additional facts and data do I need to build more credibility? What other options do I have in moving forward? There are always alternatives. What are people afraid of with my idea? What could go wrong? Have I considered these fears and doubts, and built them into my plan? Do I have a credible plan? What is it and what makes it credible?

Disbelief is a close cousin of fear. The successful zentrepreneur has to pay close attention to both. Overcoming disbelief is ultimately what wows people in a truly transformational way. Years ago, who would have believed we could land people on the moon or call someone halfway around the world on a wireless phone? Who would have believed in most of the inventions and innovations we take for granted today? Belief has to start somewhere. Without belief, there can be no passion. The zentrepreneur uses imagination and passion to inspire and zenergize people. Make no mistake, whether it is Walt Disney, Sam Walton, or Steve Jobs, passion and zenergy are contagious. People feel it when the leader is inspired. There is a spiritual and emotional connection. This goes far beyond intellect. Zenergy captures people's hearts and speaks to their souls.

Stop and examine your own doubts and limiting beliefs. Keep in mind most of these barriers are subconscious, remaining hidden from the busy mind. They are

latent, mental programs governing your habits and running your day-to-day life. They are your autopilot. To
uncover these habitual memes, take time to contemplate
and evaluate your tendencies. Meditate on them. Within
one tendency, there can be thousands of subconscious
thoughts and beliefs. Ask yourself why you think what
you think, believe what you believe, and behave the way
you do. Why do you worry about certain things? Why do
you feel anxious or stressed about thoughts that may never
happen? Why do you choose to accept these thoughts?
Why do you cling to thoughts that are painful? Why do
you not let these thoughts go? Why do you resist or deny
yourself freedom and success? Why do you talk yourself
out of things? What are your tendencies telling you about
your subconscious programming? Just beware: if your re-
sponses to any of these why questions suggest blaming
someone or something else for your shortcomings—your
genetics, your heritage, your race, your religion, your parents, your schooling, your government, your boss, your
spouse, or anyone external to you—you are subscribing
to a victim-consciousness and belief system. This itself is
a powerful meme you need to delete. Until you deal with
this potent root cause, your problems will never go away.
You will always find someone or something to blame.

The zentrepreneur takes time every day to contemplate these crucial questions and the habitual answers that
follow them. These answers can be quite revealing. We

also turn the questions and answers around as we play with them. Is there really such thing as failure if I gain from it? Is making a mistake bad if I learn a positive lesson from it? Is rejection really something to fear or gain from? Perhaps it is exactly what I need to hear at the moment to reconsider my options and sharpen my focus. Perhaps it is just what I need to grow stronger and wiser. How is this not helpful?

Zentrepreneurs take note of our own brutal facts—the good, the bad, and the ugly. What are we blessed with? What competencies and skills do we have to offer the world? Where are we limited or constrained? What hindrances and challenges do we need to overcome? What help do we need? What help can we offer? How can we best leverage our strengths and offset our limitations? More than anything, what is our "altitude" telling us about our attitude? Is it possible that we are exactly where we are supposed to be given our current level of thinking? What do we truly believe about what we can and can't do? Why do we think this way? What mental and emotional programs are governing our lives, consciously and subconsciously? Use the mirror as a metaphor for carefully examining the relationship between what we sow and what we reap. There can be no positive change in outputs without a positive change in inputs. Find the right levers and you can move the world.

When I gave my first public seminar in 1988, I invited a trusted university professional to attend the event and give me feedback. My intentions were positive, and my interest was in learning ways to improve my presentation skills. I wanted to step up my performance. I also asked the participants to complete written evaluations. The written evaluations for the seminar were very positive and I secured two new clients from the event. I had every reason to believe I did a great job. Still, I asked for candid feedback from my friend. I knew I could do better. To this day, my colleague's words echo in my mind. She simply asked me if I wanted the truth. Right there, I knew she had some constructive criticism to offer. This might hurt. Would I resist? Would I rationalize that she might be wrong by using the other positive feedback to justify my performance? Would I allow my own insecurities to skew the data and hold me back? Would I move from offense to defense? No, I wanted the truth. I wanted candid feedback. She delivered not only some very helpful ideas, but a very positive lead on where I could get some credible training on effective presentation skills and experiential learning techniques. I listened and enrolled in the workshop she suggested. I traveled to Chicago to attend the event, despite the fact that I could barely afford it. Now I reap the benefits, a return on my investment that is beyond calculation. This is the essence of zentrepreneurship. We turn good ideas into great results by listening to constructive feedback and acting on it.

Ownership, responsibility, and accountability are embedded in the zentrepreneurial mind. To successfully turn a good idea into great results, we have to own it. We have to take responsibility for it. We have to undertake the risk and be accountable for our results. The French word *entrepreneur* literally means "one who undertakes." Every entrepreneur undertakes risk. There is risk attached to everything we act on and own. For many people, this is frightening. It may seem easier to play it safe, stay on the sidelines, and let someone else take the risk. There is no room for this disempowering, external locus of control with the zentrepreneur. To be successful, we must seize the day and capitalize on the opportunities that continue to present themselves to the open, positive mind. There is no shortage of good ideas. There is only the reluctance to act, take charge, and be accountable.

Many of my clients struggle initially with taking ownership and accountability. Organizationally, culturally, and individually, there is often a tendency to shift responsibility, deny accountability, rationalize waste, and point the finger. I see it all the time. It exists in business, government, education, and healthcare. It is as if the senior leadership is inviting people to take a risk and step up, but relatively few people proactively accept the call, including many employees already in positions of management! It seems they would rather play it safe, standing on the sidelines instead of getting into the game. To me this is like going through life with the brakes on. What is holding people back? Is it fear, insecurity, doubt, disbelief? Is it ignorance, pride, ego? These are questions every change agent must contemplate, because without a true sense of ownership, the organization is paralyzed. Fear and blame are disempowering energies. Ignorance and ego are limiting factors. Insecurity and apathy are crippling beliefs. We need ownership and initiative to overcome these self-imposed constraints. Zentrepreneurs know this and do something about it.

When I was in high school, I experienced a devastating accident. I was working on a lawn-mowing crew, and I cut my foot severely with a lawn mower. Six days in the hospital and 10 hours of two surgeries later, I was told by an award-winning, internationally renowned surgeon that I would never play football again—a passion of mine at the time. In fact, he said that I would be lucky to walk again without limping. I wept with grief and remorse for days, broken-hearted at this unexpected turn of events. How could I have been so stupid? Why did this happen to me? The fact that we were the returning state champions in football and I was elected a captain of the team added even more salt to my wounds. Where would I be now when the college recruiters came to potentially offer scholarships? At age 17, I was miserable. I had really screwed up. What was I to do now?

The year was 1977, and in those days, lawn mowers did not have many of the safety features they have today. Perhaps I could argue that it was the lawn mower manufacturer's fault that my future was doomed? In a very litigious society, there are certainly many who might agree. Why not shift the blame to someone else? Maybe it was the homeowner's fault? After all, she asked me to cut down a stretch of tall field grass along the side her house so that she could throw a lawn party. This was not part of our original deal and the tall grass was full of rocks, one of which I tripped over. Maybe I could blame the rock? Or maybe I could blame the surgeon, despite his competence and credibility. Maybe he should have done a better job fixing my foot. Or maybe I could blame my shoes or my lawn-crew partner or the stars?

Truth be told, I owned the problem. It was my foot, my doing, my life, my future. It was my choice to play victim or champion. I stood at a mystical fork in the road called life, and I had to decide which way to go. What do I choose? How do I respond to this test of character? I chose ownership. I opted to take charge and be responsible for moving forward in a positive way, not wallowing in grief or self-pity over something I could not undo. The past is past. There is no sense in reliving it. I had to let go. I had to opt for the path of optimism, opportunity, and prosperity. Three years later, I was playing football for the

University of Notre Dame, tapping a sign on Saturdays that reads "Play like a champion today."

Zentrepreneurs do not give up easily, and the only activities we procrastinate are the things that don't really matter. Those low-impact activities can wait for another day. We set priorities and recognize that initiative and perseverance are critical success factors to manifesting any good idea. We use intuition to connect the dots and find solutions where others see problems. These characteristics and tendencies are inherent in every zentrepreneur. We are catalysts and finishers. We get things started and we get things done. Handoffs are seamless and fumbles are rare, because we manage the gaps carefully. Most of the time we make forward movement, and when we make mistakes, we learn from them. It is this positive outlook and forward movement that inspire people, including the zentrepreneur. Zenergy generates zenergy.

Optimism is a quality we all have available to us if we choose to let go of pessimism. It is the yang on the other side of yin. It is a simple choice but a massive change in habit—leading to profound differences in perspective. Is the glass half full or half empty? What do you see? What are your tendencies telling you about your subconscious thinking? When people see problems, do you agree? Do you fall in line with the norm? Or do you see opportunities in disguise, possibilities waiting to be discovered?

When people see scarcity, do you see abundance? When people see failure, do you see the lessons being learned? Paying attention to contrast and context is what leads to wisdom. Once again, what do you see? Your mindset makes all the difference.

One of my favorite stories is the tale of Thomas Edison being interviewed by a journalist. The reporter allegedly asked how he could continue his efforts after more than 9,000 failed attempts at the light bulb. Wasn't this discouraging? Edison replied that he hadn't failed yet. He had learned more than 9,000 ways that didn't work. What a great example of zentrepreneurship and the power of positive thinking!

If your idea is not selling or working, ask yourself why. Contemplate it with an open mind. Do a Force Field Analysis. Look at it from different perspectives and ask for candid feedback. Chances are *you* probably have something to do with it. You might be the one who has to change. You might be the constraint. You might be the one in the way. It might be you who has to get out of your own way. Learn from it, make your adjustments, and move on. There is always room for improvement.

Checklist for Success

- I question the value of my ideas, asking why are they important and relevant.

- I use facts and data to challenge my assumptions, fears, and doubts.

- I aim projects and solutions at root causes, not effects.

- I do my homework to build credibility and help sell my ideas.

- I know my audience and the forces against me.

- I am proactive, optimistic, and positive. I give off good zenergy!

- I accept ownership, responsibility, and accountability for my ideas and actions.

- I look in the mirror first when things go wrong.

- I ask "Why?" A lot!

3

Why Not?

A man's mind stretched to a new idea never goes back to its original dimensions.

—Oliver Wendell Holmes

In 1992, an idea came my way. What if I write a book? I had already written several workbooks and training manuals. I was in the consulting profession, similar to the "publish or perish" profession of higher education. It made sense to write a book. The reasons to do so were quite compelling: It could help me reach more people, enhance my credibility, and lead to more recognition in the industry. It could help me differentiate myself from other consultants, supplement my income, and contribute to my retirement. It could become part of my legacy. There were many good reasons for me to pursue this idea.

The creative thinker asks not just "Why?" but "Why not?" There are two sides to every coin, and multiple options and solutions to every problem. Often, the first "right" answer is not the best answer. To apply zentrepreneurial thinking effectively, we must learn to ask questions in a variety of different ways. With the question "Why not?" we can look at the ideas from a different perspective. What are the risks? What could go wrong? What is the cost of doing nothing? What are the forces for and against the idea? What are the primary obstacles to overcome in order for the idea to be successful? What is missing?

By asking "why not," I uncovered several risks associated with the idea:

- I did not know how to write a book.

- I did not have an agent.

- I did not have a publisher.

- I had very limited time and resources to invest in the project.

- I was told by a former boss that I was not a good writer.

Using the Force Field Analysis tool, I weighed the forces for and against the idea, and then looked into what it would take to develop "countermeasures" for the forces against me. In other words, what could I do to offset or mitigate the risks? What do the data and analysis really tell me about pursuing the idea? Clearly, I did not want to waste my time and resources and neither did anyone else. My homework continued when my sister gave me a book on how to write and publish a book. This book walked me through the various options I had step by step and proved to be immensely valuable. I now had a deeper understanding of what I had to do to be successful at writing and publishing a book. Put simply, I read a book on how to write a book.

I continued to be met with resistance and unacceptable terms from agents and publishers "passing" on my preliminary proposals or taking too long to get the work published, so I eventually self-published my first book in 1993 and my second book in 1994. This is where the intuition, initiative, perseverance, optimism, and belief come into play. Zentrepreneurs find a way to get things done, and we tend to work fast. This is also where we tend to make some mistakes. In this case, I could have spent a little more time doing my homework and gathering more data. I will never forget sitting in a book publishing conference in Orlando, Florida, in 1995. This was a conference aimed at helping authors, publishers, literary agents, editors, book marketers, and distributors by providing wise and experienced counsel on the industry and its practices.

As a relatively young author now with two self-published books, I figured it might offer me some very useful and profitable tricks of the trade. During the conference, several concurrent workshops were held allowing authors to meet with publishing experts to get feedback on their work. The feedback on my first two books was simple: I did a lot of things wrong! My book covers were not industry savvy. There were no bar codes on the cover. The books didn't "look right." I had a weak marketing and distribution plan. The list went on and on. In fact, the only thing the experts could not really explain is how the books sold out so fast. My first printing of 3,000 copies sold in less than a year. In fact, that first book, titled *Pulling Together: The Power of Teamwork*, still sells widely on Amazon.com. It also got the attention of Mac Anderson, who now has an abbreviated version of the book on Simple Truths Top-10 best-seller list. It was also a best-seller for Successories. What would the world be like without mistakes!

Think carefully about this. Why not pursue your idea? What could go wrong? How serious would it be if it did go wrong? How likely is it that it will go wrong? Ultimately, what are the risks associated with your idea? What are the risks of *not* pursuing your idea? Look at it both ways. Invite others to critique the idea and provide you with candid feedback. Ask for pushback. Do not resist it! Open your mind and heart to the wisdom and experience of others. Zentrepreneurs tend to surround themselves with wise counsel and advisors.

No one is successful alone. Arrogance and stubbornness obstruct flow. Resistance to help is not helpful. A strong defense without a strong offense is not enough to win championships. Protecting the status quo does not foster creativity, fearlessness, innovation, and advancement. It grounds us in the past. It is unnatural and often quite destructive.

What kind of advice do you listen to? Where is it coming from? Do you check your sources? Do you check your source's sources? Are you aware that some alleged "experts" are very quick to give advice about subjects they know very little about? And there are plenty of people asking for it and listening to it—without considering the facts! Pay attention to who and what you pay attention to.

The question "Why not?" helps us gain insight, credibility, and intelligence. It is a question that challenges our assumptions and helps us prepare for more effective planning. If we don't ask it ourselves, someone else likely will. If we haven't thought through the potential risks, invaluable credibility can be lost. We set ourselves up for the "oops syndrome." This does not mean we will not make mistakes—we will. It simply helps us avoid many careless and costly mishaps that are reasonably predictable.

Successful zentrepreneurs contemplate the many reasons why a good idea may not manifest into great results. Some of these reasons include:

- Poor marketing and service.

- Limited capital.

- Operational constraints.

- Ego and control issues.

- No teamwork or support.

- Ignorance.

Marketing is absolutely fundamental to business and success. It starts with awareness and credibility. Are key people and markets even aware of your idea or value proposition? How do they—or how will they—know about you and what you have to offer? Are you "Google-able?" Are you visible and easy to find? How does your value proposition align with your target market's interests, desires, and needs? Who is your audience and what do you really know about them? Who are your customers' customers? What problems are they trying to solve? What alternatives do they have? What kind of competition are you up against? How is your solution different? How do you know?

Zentrepreneurs know and apply certain marketing practices that most people do not. This is what differentiates us from the pack. This is what keeps us moving forward on the leading edge of innovation and change, forcing others to catch up. We do things that *exceed* customer expectations. We solve problems before the customer even knows there is a problem, and fill latent needs before the customer knows they have a need. We offer value propositions that seem impossible, yet we deliver on our word. We understand that the customer is *not* always right, that the customer often does not know what they want until they see it. As Lee Iacocca put it many years ago, no one ever came to Chrysler and asked for a mini-van to be designed. Zentrepreneurs understand that the customer may *not* be "the next one down the line" in the supply chain and that many internal customers have no idea what the true end-user really values. Without understanding who the real customers are and clearly defining value in the eyes of the end-users, we have little chance of consistently getting it right. We simply offer things that require time and resources but have little positive impact on the people who ultimately pay for it.

Truly effective marketing requires "wowing" people. Zentrepreneurs see customer service not as a department, but as an attitude. It is a belief system, habit, and culture. It is a collective way of seeing the world.

Wowing customers is not a one-off exception; it is the rule. Exceeding expectations is not a surprise; rather, it is planned and executed with diligence, ease, and grace. Meeting obvious customer needs is good. This is what customer *satisfaction* is all about. It is like going on a blind date with someone and telling your friends afterwards that it was "satisfactory." Not much passion and enthusiasm here. In fact, some studies show that 68 percent of satisfied customers will take their business somewhere else when a better offer comes along. This is not customer loyalty, and it is certainly not customer advocacy.

Customer advocates (those customers who are so impressed that they rave about your company to others) are consistently wowed, not because obvious needs are met, but because they are offered solutions to problems they don't even know they have. We had no idea what the Internet, Google, or the iPad could do for us until we experienced them. And when we experienced them, we had little to say but "Wow!" Now, with the touch of a button or the click of a mouse, we can download books, reserve seats at a show, get directions to a restaurant, or book an airline seat on a specific flight.

Who ordered barcodes, RFID chips, MRI scans, and wireless technology? Who decided online banking was a good idea? Was it the customer? Why would Amazon imagine, design, create, and pioneer a Kindle—an alternative to physical books and bookstores—when selling books is what originally put the company on the map? Does this seem odd? Why potentially put your original business out of business by making one of your mainstream products obsolete? The answer may not be so secretive anymore. If we do not think on the leading edge and challenge old paradigms, our competition will eat our lunch. Sooner or later, someone else will change the rules and set us back to zero. The race of innovation is ongoing and endless. Customers like being wowed. There is no shortage of need for zentrepreneurship.

When Chrysler sent engineers out to grocery store parking lots to observe people (predominately mothers with children) trying to load groceries into the side of a car in tight parking spaces, they uncovered an opportunity—latent needs that their customers had but never commented on. They saw the need for sliding doors and a vehicle that was not quite so low to the ground. They conceived the original mini-van, a true blockbuster.

Amazon and others are now doing the same thing with books. Just take five minutes to examine the contents and weight of a child's school backpack. Better yet, take a look at the price of some of these textbooks, particularly in college. Why not just beam the books through thin air to a lightweight template that does a thousand other things for you as well? Why not lighten the load, reduce the costs, save some trees, and reduce the carbon footprint all at the same time?

The world is awakening to a field of completely new possibilities and opportunities. Zentrepreneurs seek to get there first and effective marketing plays a key role. Pay close attention to your target market or audience. What are they struggling with? Where is the waste and clutter in the relationship? What is distracting or getting in the way? What is frustrating or annoying people?

Do not ask if everything is okay (and hope to hear yes). This is a first-level question that tells you very little. It is like asking a child how his day was. Chances are, you will hear a first-level answer like "fine" or "okay," which tells you nothing. Get out and observe people. Order your own products. Experience what other people are experiencing. Seek to learn what is wrong, difficult, or missing in the market. Here is where you will find some of the subtle secrets to zentrepreneurship and great results.

Another reason why a good idea may not manifest into great results is limited capital. It is often easier to get something started than to actually see it through to harvest. Money is the lifeblood of business. It is the currency, the flow. It is what allows us to invest in growth and it is what pays the bills. Zentrepreneurs get this. We understand the importance of cash flow. We pay attention to returns on investments, balance sheets, and profit and loss statements. Taking your eye off the ball on monetary and fiscal responsibility is a dangerous risk. Pay attention to the numbers. Establish budgets and stick to them. Know your limitations. Be resourceful.

I started my consulting company in 1988 with a ready-to-assemble desk, a computer, a printer, and a phone. I also invested in marketing material such as letterhead stationery, business cards, and brochures, and I contracted an answering service to respond to phone calls with live service. Later I added some ready-to-assemble bookshelves to house my growing library. In contrast, a friend of mine was starting a consulting firm at the same time. He chose to lease office space in the city center, furnish it with expensive furniture, hire an administrative assistant, and make a big splash. His company did not survive. This does not mean that it couldn't have. The successful zentrepreneur thinks "creativity before capital." Lean thinking is a key to turning good ideas into great results. Money matters, so be sure to make wise use of it. Sometimes less gives us more! Need is often the mother of invention and innovation.

One of my great challenges getting started in business was the combination of these first two critical success factors: poor marketing and limited capital. I had no marketing department, no sales force, and very little money, so I was limited on my capacity to market and sell my services—or so I thought. The zentrepreneur never gives up on a good idea at the first sign of defeat. We continue to ask why and why not. We also use a creativity technique called reverse questioning. Disney, an incredibly creative culture, is masterful at using techniques like this. At Disney, the mission is "to make people happy," so an example of a reverse question is "What makes people unhappy?" The answers to this question then become the true competition, the forces against us. The question also reveals opportunities that are in our control so we can actually do something about them.

In my case, I had to ask how I could market my business and services with less money, not more money. How could I mail brochures and make sales calls at zero cost—or perhaps even make money doing it? How could I get people in the market to know about my services and subsidize the marketing costs? How could I get prospects to come to me rather than me go to them? Keep in mind, this was in 1988, and the Internet and social media were still untapped. Common practice in those days was to make a lot of sales calls requiring excessive time, travel, and material. I found most of this practice to be wasteful and expensive.

Reverse questions led me to new ideas. What if I offered a workshop or seminar? What if I "invested" in a mailer that didn't just get filed away or trashed? What if the mailer actually invited prospects to come learn something new for a reasonable fee? Perhaps I could send out hundreds and maybe even thousands of brochures, and get the costs covered by people paying to come learn something? Surely there was risk in this idea, but if I scoped it to a small target market and piloted it within a strict budget, it would be a risk worth taking. It was this thought process that resulted in my first public workshop, my first workbook, my first clients, and eventually my first book. Within two years, I was offering workshops nationwide with multiple mailings of tens of thousands at a time.

Operational constraints are another critical success factor the zentrepreneur must be aware of. Assuming the marketing and financial factors are covered, we think about what else could go wrong. We have a brand, awareness, customers, demand, orders, and cash flow. The key question now is, Can we deliver? Can we execute? Can we live up to our promises? Can we meet our deadlines? What is our true capacity to wow people and create customer advocates? After all, delighted customers are our most credible salespeople, and it doesn't cost us anything to have them out recommending us. When they rave to their families and friends about the great experience they have had with our company, people listen. There is no hidden agenda.

Take a good look at what you can and can't do for your market or audience. Avoid making promises you cannot keep just to make the sale. Beware of digging yourself into a financial hole you cannot climb out of. Identify your operational constraints and plan accordingly. What are your limitations? What are your core competencies, and how can you exploit these? Where are your weaknesses, and how can you offset these? Do you have the talent you need? Do you have the resources you need? Do you have the equipment you need? Do you have the time you need? These are all important "why nots" that need to be contemplated and addressed. A lot of ideas get crushed not because they are not good ideas, but because the execution fails.

Ego and control issues frequently contribute to the demise of many good ideas. Often the entrepreneur gets in his or her own way. Rather than let go and let flow, the ego interferes. The ego is a fear-based, dualistic thought system that reveals the "false self." It is the insecure self. It is what triggers fear, doubt, separation, jealousy, anger, control, and pride. It is what keeps many people from recognizing their true identity, their true spiritual essence. Beyond ego, we are fearless, infinite spiritual beings. The zentrepreneur embraces the authentic Self, recognizing that we have extraordinary power available to us that we can use to create, grow, innovate, and evolve when we let go of the obstacles holding it back.

There are no shortages of ideas and opportunities in this world, and there are no problems without solutions. The only real limitation is the false self, the fearful, dualistic personality that seeks separation, competition, and control.

Successful zentrepreneurs value cooperation over competition, and interdependent teamwork over independent ego. We know that in order to be highly successful with our ideas, we need commitment and support from others. We need people to coach us. We need people to advise us, challenge us, reinforce our ideas, and fill in the gaps that inevitably show up. Teamwork is a powerful success factor. The ability to pull people together, focus and align behavior, and allow zenergy to amplify synergy is essential to turning good ideas into great results.

As a business consultant and executive coach, I am challenged every week to manifest good ideas into exemplary results. I do this *through* people, not *to* people. In fact, I have no positional authority at all with any of my clients. The only power I have is the power of influence. Yet, every week, we continue to make gains, because we clear the air of fear and doubt. We use kaizen events to pull people together and get things done— fast! We work in teams where everyone has a chance to express their ideas and concerns, and we act on these ideas quickly when the risk is assessed and the expected return looks good.

The "zen" in kaizen is powerful. These events are not just about changing methods, documents, policies, processes, or procedures. They are about changing minds. They are about inspiring creativity and human potential. They are about breeding commitment—the heart and soul of teamwork. When facilitated effectively, people see things differently. Paradigms, assumptions, and perceptions shift. It is not unusual to hear team members say "A-ha!" and "Wow!" during an event and express a desire to do additional kaizen events later on. The zentrepreneur leverages this social and human capital to manifest great results.

Sometimes our competition is not who we think it is. The typical paradigm in business is that the competition is some other company trying to take our business or some other person trying to take our job. It is a component of capitalism, and it is built on the platform of ego, fear, separation, and scarcity. The zentrepreneur recognizes this common model and sees past it. Competition can be healthy and wise, but it can also be limiting and destructive. It can result in win-lose conflicts when win-win alternatives exist. It is wise to beware of this. Win-lose results can come back and haunt us.

In my line of work, it is not uncommon for me to partner with other consulting firms to deliver value to our clients. We do this all the time. In some circles, people might see this cooperation as conflictive. Many of the consultants and firms I work with offer exactly the same services I do. We could be viewed as competitors. Yet we frequently pull each other in, when need be, to take care of our clients. This gives us a very flexible, cooperative, virtual model that other firms find hard to compete with. It is a zentrepreneurial model where the best interests of the client keep us focused and aligned as a team. This model also gives us a wonderful opportunity to share ideas and learn from one another, a true win-win for us and the clients.

Ignorance is not bliss. It is a form of blindness. In Zen practice, the word *buddha* means "awake." Zen is a form of enlightenment, peace, equanimity, higher awareness, and pure consciousness. When we wake up from ego and ignorance, we realize we didn't know what we didn't know. We were in the dark. We were missing certain facts and discoveries. We were the blind being led by the blind—and perhaps leading the blind. This may feel like bliss, but in business it is a recipe for disaster. To run a successful business, we need to shift from "I think" to "I know" in every possible way. We need to shift from assumption to fact, from data to information, and from intellect to intelligence. Many business leaders do not know the difference.

Stop and ask yourself if you truly know, with accurate facts and intelligence, what your customer is experiencing with your products or services. Do you truly know, or do you *think* you know? Do you know your right-first-time (RFT) yields? Do you know your cycle times? Do you know your inventory turns? Do you know your constraints? Do you know the challenges your team is facing every day? Do you know best practices? Do you know better ways to do what you do? Do you know how you compare to your competition? Do you know what new technologies are available? Do you truly know what your boss thinks or what your employees think about your performance? The list of contemplative questions goes on and on. The brutal reality is this: when we let go of ego, insecurity, and false pride, we discover we really do not know much about anything with absolute certainty. We only think we do. Zentrepreneurs keep an open, humble mind. We practice the wisdom of emptiness, meaning we empty our "bowl" in order for it to be refilled. We admit we don't know what we don't know. A closed mind can learn no more. This is what makes the journey of discovery so fascinating. It is a process of awakening.

Checklist for Success

- I keep an open, humble mind.

- I contemplate my options without judgment.

- I do not stop looking with the first "right" answer.

- I ask reverse questions to stimulate creativity.

- I assess and mitigate the risks of my ideas and options.

- I seek insights and advice from wise counsel.

- I pay attention to my audience and customers, seeking the wow factor.

- I surround myself with a good team.

- I let go of ego and let flow with Spirit.

- I ask "Why not?" A lot!

4

Who?

Never doubt that a small group of thoughtful, committed people can change the world. Indeed, it is the only thing that ever has.

—Margaret Mead

In 1994, a good idea came my way. It was offered to me from a dear friend and trusted advisor, Elizabeth Jennings. Betty had just finished reading my book *Agent of Change: Leading a Cultural Revolution*, and she said to me, "John, you know you have to write a sequel to this book." I replied, "I do?" She went on to explain the many reasons why I should follow this advice, including the timeliness and need for such a book in the market. People all over the country were struggling with corporate restructurings, downsizings, job eliminations, and career uncertainties. This book could offer creative insights and practical ideas to millions of people on how to turn employment lemons into lemonade. With my background in human resources management, organizational development, career counseling, and management consulting, she suggested that I had just what was needed to write such a book. It would be the perfect next step following *Agent of Change*, a story about how a general manager transformed his company culture. To do this, the GM had to make some very difficult decisions, including the dismissal of a key manager who refused to get on board. I listened, asked why and why not, played with the idea, and assessed the risk. And in 1995, *Reinvent Yourself: A Lesson in Personal Leadership* was born. This book, a story written from the dismissed manager's point of view, then got the attention of Dale Dauten, a syndicated writer who highly recommended it in his column as "soulful and a good read." Soon it was helping people all over North America. The book also helped me to see the vital connection between Spirit and work, awakening me to a whole new level of opportunity and promise. Writing it was indeed a soulful adventure.

Zentrepreneurs are team players. We surround ourselves with capable, competent, trusted allies. True success is not something we do alone. Winning championships requires teamwork. Look behind any great athlete and you will find great coaching. Look beside any wise leader and you will find wise counsel. Look in front of any successful student and you will find effective teachers and mentors. We all belong to a world that is significantly larger than any one of us. Our ability to build healthy relationships and network with people in a win-win way is fundamental to success. Who really knows what may come of it? Who knows what ideas may spring forth? Who knows what our neighbors might know, or who they might know? We live in a small world with big ideas. Are we paying attention to the people we meet and the ideas they share? Are we really listening?

I feel fortunate to be able to work with people all over the world in a variety of different industries, cultures, environments, and circumstances. What amazes me are the extraordinary hidden talents that surface once people feel "safe" to speak up and share their insights, ideas, and experiences. In virtually every project and kaizen event, I meet people who have good ideas but struggle with getting the great results. Often this is because it is tough for a single individual to take on the overall system and culture. Many organizations, like people, are set in their ways. In most cases, it takes a team of committed people, a constituency for change, to influence and effect the establishment. This is what zentrepreneurs and kaizen events are all about. We build these constituencies for change. We develop a collective mind. We share a vision. We take ownership for making the change and being accountable for the results. There is power in numbers. There is synergy in teamwork.

When I look back over the years, I am not sure I have done anything alone. Even a process like writing a book, seemingly independent, is a collaborative effort. We need ideas, examples, editors, artists, designers, marketers, distributors, agents, publishers, retailers, and readers to make it work. In my consulting work, I do not make changes to my clients. I make changes *with* them. As a teacher, I recognize the ancient wisdom in the saying "When the student is ready, the teacher will appear." I cannot teach effectively without attentive students. I cannot communicate effectively without an open audience. We all rely on each other for one thing or another, and it is foolish and arrogant to think we can do it alone.

As an executive coach, I work with a lot of well-educated, well-paid people. Some are wise and emotionally secure. Others are not. The assumption some people make here is that these people are all successful. They have all earned their way to the top. They all make big bucks. They all have academic degrees. They are the leaders. They know what they are doing. Why would they need a coach? Why would they pay for additional help?

Here is the reality: the best of the best have great counsel. The wise pay attention to the wise. People who suffer most are people who deny and resist the need for competent help, people trapped by an insecure, false identity of self—the ego. An arrogant know-it-all resists coaching because he fears it will reveal ignorance. An over-confident controller resists counsel because she fears it will uncover weakness and incompetence. Fear is a formidable foe when it comes to stepping up. It takes courage and wisdom to be a true team player, and courage requires that we let go of the illusion of security and control. We lead change by taking risks.

Zentrepreneurs are opportunists. We listen for good ideas and then we look for ways to translate them into great results. We listen to people. We get away from our desks and "go see where the work is done." In Japan, this is referred to as *gemba*, the action zone. We pay attention to what people want and need. We notice what aggravates and annoys people. We seek solutions to problems many people do not even know they have. We explore new ground with an eye for continuous improvement. We seek to make change, not manage it or resist it. We find ways to go with the flow, not against it. We use zenergy to pull people together, not push them apart. We use diversity to our advantage and honor people's differences. We recognize that, without contrast, we could not understand content. What is hot if there is no cold? What is up if there is no down? What is peace if there is no conflict? We need to experience darkness to know light. We need to experience illness to appreciate health. All is in perfect yin-yang harmony and balance, and we are wise to flow with the power of life rather than against it. This means sowing positive seeds to reap productive harvests. It means building positive relationships to generate healthy teamwork. It means involving, aligning, and empowering team members to accelerate results. We pay attention to the inputs to improve the outputs.

One of the most common tools we use for leading change is the IPO Diagram. This relatively simple tool helps teams correlate inputs and outputs. Think of it like baking a cake. Clearly, we need the proper ingredients to get desirable results. We also need clear and accurate instructions, reliable equipment and instrumentation, proven methods, and well-trained, capable people. These are all critical inputs. Variation with any of these inputs (x) will propagate to the outputs (y), potentially causing undesirable effects. If the cake is to taste good, look good, be on time, and be affordable, we have to master the transfer function: $y=f(x)$. Obviously, the variables will be different if we are attempting to put a satellite in space rather than bake a cake. Either way, every process has inputs and outputs. The secret to success is in understanding what the critical inputs are and what the relationship is between the inputs and outputs. Keep in mind that within each general input category, like material or people, there can be many more specific inputs to explore, such as the exact materials, documents, and components we are using, the source of these materials and documents, the neccessary level of competency and training, the needed level of staffing to support demand, the clarity and effectiveness of the reporting structure, and so on.

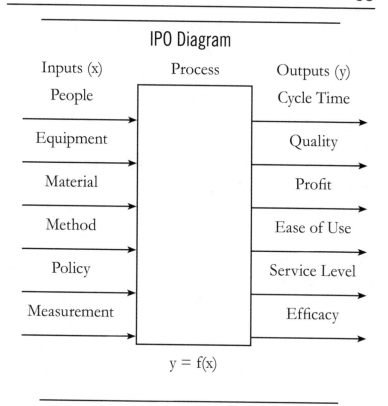

One of the most important factors in successfully leading culture change is the people. We are highly variable. We have different talents, perceptions, experiences, habits, and ideas. The zentrepreneur welcomes this diversity, recognizing that it contributes to what I call the genius of the team. When we work alone, we make assumptions that often go unchallenged. We are limited by our own perceptions, experiences, beliefs, and paradigms, many of which are hidden at the subconscious level of the mind. However, when we are working with a team of capable people, we will be challenged if our perceptions and ideas do not seem to make sense. This is the classic "storming" stage of teamwork. We do not all see things the same way. This is a blessing, not a curse. It is what leads to synergy if we manage it effectively. It is then our ability to pull people together, focus the team on common interests, and create alignment that manifests high-performance results. Zenergy can only be generated when we are all moving in the same direction. Zenergy is transformative. The zentrepreneur knows that there is a fifth stage of teamwork, beyond the traditional four: form, storm, norm, perform—and transform! It is at the transformational level that true, sustainable culture change has taken place. Team members feel like champions because they have evidence that they are. The high performance team expects to win. Fear, hope, misalignment, and doubt have been transcended and replaced by quiet self-assurance, trust, and empowering belief. Great coaches make believers out of people.

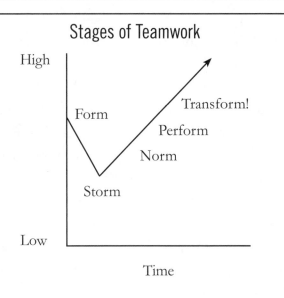

The transformational power of kaizen events is extraordinary. What takes many companies months and even years to accomplish with one-hour weekly meetings, we can accomplish in a week with the right people in the right room, with the right level of expertise and authority. The "who" makes a huge difference. However, this key factor is not always understood. In one kaizen event I was facilitating in Portugal, we discovered on Monday that the customer had sent an administrative person to be a representative. This particular event was intended to identify and make immediate changes to improve process flow, and reduce unnecessary handling and rework between my client and this customer. When we realized we did not have the necessary authority in the room to approve the recommendations immediately, we had to improvise. We asked the administrative representative if she could arrange for us to visit the customer on Wednesday to present our recommendations on process improvement. She was able to schedule us an appointment for Wednesday afternoon, which gave us two days to prepare. We went immediately to work, drafted the changes, developed a prototype for approval, rented a bus, and met with the customer to get approval. As it turned out, they loved the changes we proposed, and we got the go-ahead to implement immediately. The who matters when it comes to making decisions and taking action, sooner not later. It is important to get the right people involved with the right level of authority to get things done efficiently and effectively.

In another kaizen event in 2009, we put a team from Lyon, France, on a plane and flew to Windsor, England, to improve a key process shared between a vendor (my client) and a customer. Put simply, the two independent systems were not working well together interdependently, and this was causing a great deal of expensive and time-consuming rework. Prior to our visit, we planned the event, who would participate in it, and what would be required in terms of preliminary data gathering and process mapping. When we arrived in England, we got right to work searching for win-win solutions and building a constituency for change. By Friday, we had approval to go ahead with the improvements. This resulted in millions of dollars in savings and improvements for my client's customer—which meant a nice win for my client as well. It even led to a "Top 10 Supplier of the Year Award" from the customer, a very large company with more than 10,000 different suppliers. The improvement also led to a nice increase in orders for my client.

There are no shortages of good ideas. They exist everywhere, surrounding us like high-frequency radio waves. Just because we do not hear them does not mean they are not there. It may simply mean that we are not tuned into them. Music is playing all the time. In fact, all different kinds of music are playing right now along with talk radio, athletic contests, news, and other channels. We need to open ourselves up to the zenergy and frequency that are available to us. As I mentioned earlier, I do this with techniques like meditation and contemplation. I also do this by paying close attention to people, learning their names, asking for their ideas and insights, and seeking value in what they offer. Rather than resist new ideas and new relationships, I build on them.

My book *Reinvent Yourself* came from an idea Elizabeth Jennings offered me. I did not plan this. I simply listened and executed. This book actually led to another sequel and then a prequel. Go figure. My first book, *Pulling*

Together, captured the attention of Mac Anderson, founder of two very successful companies, Successories and Simple Truths. Mac first asked me if I could write a condensed version of *Pulling Together* for Successories, which I did, and later he asked if I could write a gift book version of it for Simple Truths. Both became best-sellers for these two companies, a win-win-win for the publishers, the readers, and the writer. The ideas did not come from me, they came through me.

I apply the same team practice to my consulting business. When I started the company in 1988, I brought in two partners. We developed a plan and set out to make it work. Not all good ideas manifest into great results. In this case, both of my partners elected to leave the business within the first year. It was a much rougher start than we anticipated, and they both needed to leave for valid reasons. We were selling "change management" before it was vogue, and we were not prepared for the resistance we initially met in the marketplace. Both partners left on good terms, and I had to improvise quickly to keep the business alive. I was not willing to give up. During that same year, I attended an executive education program at the University of Michigan Graduate Business School, where I met a fellow student who would later become a good friend and colleague. We continued to stay in touch, and years later, we found ourselves working together on many large consulting assignments. By networking, collaborating, and sharing best practices, we have positioned ourselves to provide services to some of the world's largest organizations, including Lockheed Martin, Raytheon, GSK, and the United States Navy.

Take time to consider who you surround yourself with. Who is part of your virtual team? Who is supplying you with good ideas? Who is helping you build on these ideas? Who is challenging these ideas and helping you with the "why not"? Who is bringing diversity to your team? Where are you limited, and who is helping you fill these gaps? Who is coaching you and providing you with candid feedback and wise counsel? Who are you listening to? Do they really know what they are talking about? How do you know? Are they offering you rational support or irrational encouragement? What kind of peer pressure are you experiencing? Is it high-frequency, positive zenergy or low-frequency fear, doubt, and distrust?

The Law of Attraction is a powerful law. Unfortunately, it is frequently misunderstood by people looking for a quick fix. Essentially, this universal spiritual law states that what we sow is what we reap. Put another way, we get exactly what we ask for—energetically. The essence of that which is like itself is drawn. Like energy attracts like energy. We become what we dwell on. We attract what we are and we are what we feel, which is influenced by what we think. This works both ways. When we think good things, we feel good. When we think bad things, we feel bad. Misery loves company and success breeds success. Notice this when you observe who zentrepreneurs surround themselves with. We connect with positive people, not whiners and complainers. We attract people who are part of the solution, not part of the problem. In fact, the skeptical critic often seems to take pleasure in passing judgment on the zentrepreneur, which matters not at all to the zentrepreneur. We can only be responsible for what we think, not what others think. Being mindful of this is a powerful strategy for success.

Recognize that the Law of Attraction exists whether you believe it or not, see it or not, or like it or not. It is karma. It is what keeps everything in a perfect universal yin-yang balance. Wise leaders use the law to attract a better world. We use it to turn good ideas into great results. We use it to create a culture of innovation and fearlessness. By letting go of resistance, denial, skepticism, anxiety, fear, doubt, and the negative energies that attract negative results, we free ourselves to experience the other side of the equation—the positive outcomes. We let go to let flow. We attract can-do attitudes. We appeal to people who want to help, and draw into our lives creativity, charisma, and support. We do not force this, but simply allow it by removing our own mental and emotional barriers. This is counterintuitive for many strong leaders because the idea of letting go seems like surrender. It feels like giving up. On the contrary, if we are being dragged under water by a heavy weight, we are wise to let it go. The same is true if we are clinging to a hot electrical wire or a destructive relationship with someone we love. Sometimes the very things killing us are the toughest to let go of. This includes disempowering thoughts, harmful habits, and judgmental people.

In 1995, the head of human resources for a meat-processing company contacted me to discuss providing team-building training to the management staff. I met with her and the head of operations, and we explored the "what if," the "why" and "why not." I found myself intrigued by some of the current expectations, results, and perceptions they shared. Put simply, they offered some team-building training a year earlier, and it did not work. It must have been the trainer's fault. Employee turnover was still more than 400 percent per year! New hires would often come on board and leave at first break, never to return. Meat-packing plants are not ideal work environments. More than 50 percent of the production workforce was there less than a year. The "who" was a huge problem for this company. We needed to try again.

Einstein once described insanity as doing the same thing over and over, and expecting different results. I knew one thing: I did not want to be the next scapegoat for this company. Until they took ownership and responsibility for changing the systems, the structure, and "the way we do things around here," the culture would not change. Indeed, the culture is "the way we do things around here," and it is synonymous with systems and structure. If we want to create a culture of innovation and fearlessness, we have to design it into the daily operating system with appropriate methods, metrics, and incentives. It must be a habit, not an act.

After listening to the two leaders of this meat-processing company explain the situation, I quickly discerned that training alone would not solve the problem. Sending people to team-building training, only to return to a non-team system and culture, would not work. I suggested that what they really needed was an overhaul of many of the systems they had in place, including hiring, orientating, training, developing, positioning, scheduling, incenting, rewarding, and promoting. There were also some cross-functional structural changes they could explore to reduce many of the dysfunctional behaviors they were experiencing. My suggestions caught them a bit off-guard, especially when I turned down the opportunity to provide the training. I did not see it as a win-win solution.

A few days later, I received a call from the CEO of the meat-processing company. He asked for a meeting with me and was particularly interested in discussing an article I had left behind with his two managers. The article was about one of his competitors and how the company had transformed its culture, teaching "buffaloes to fly." Metaphorically, buffalo herds have only one alpha leader. There is no self-direction, no self-management, no true empowerment. Geese, on the other hand, take turns leading. They are adaptive and team-oriented. They look out for each other and know that they gain efficiencies when they are aligned. To transform this competitor's culture, they had to teach buffaloes to behave like geese.

The article struck a note with this CEO, and he was curious about how he might accomplish the same thing with his company. Intuitively and practically, he knew that throwing more training at the problem would not resolve it. He needed to change habits, individually and organizationally. We agreed to a deal that required his support in challenging and changing the culture, including the systems and structure that held the current behaviors in place. With the help of numerous kaizen teams and events, we went to work, providing team training as one of the many inputs that needed attention. We put in a cross-functional "air traffic control" center, integrating planning, scheduling, procurement, and logistics. We took ownership for interviewing and hiring employees directly, rather than through multiple temp agencies. We designed and developed a "pay for knowledge and skill" system to reward employees for cross-training and sharing their knowledge. We overhauled the maintenance department. There were no sacred cows. We challenged everything, using data and analysis to ground ourselves in reality and confront the waste. Ideas for improvement continued to flow, and within 12 months, employee turnover was down to 5 percent per month and productivity was skyrocketing.

My children often ask me about the various companies and people I work with—especially when I came home with really tasty sausage from this client! One year I might be working with rocket scientists and technical wizards. Another year I might be working with military generals and admirals, hospital administrators, doctors, political leaders, Fortune 100 CEOs, mechanics, and sausage-makers; it is no wonder my children are curious. They also ask about the various countries I work in and the languages spoken. On one occasion I was headed off to China to facilitate a kaizen event for a sewing machine manufacturer and my oldest daughter asked if I could speak Chinese. I told her I knew two words: *please* and *thank you*. I have learned the same two words in many different languages, respecting my audience and relying heavily on translators to help me out. I explained to my children that I am not a rocket scientist, a chemist, a doctor, a mechanic, or any of the many professions I work with. These skills are valuable and important and I respect them. We need technical knowledge in every kaizen event. We need people with diverse interests and skills. We need people with ideas and the passion to see them through to manifestation. We need the "who" to make everything happen. The zentrepreneur conducts the orchestra.

Checklist for Success

- I am a team player.

- I surround myself with capable, competent people.

- I am open to diverse points of view.

- I do not need to know it all.

- I do not need to control everything.

- I see crisis as opportunity.

- I focus on the inputs to get desirable outputs.

- I lead by example.

- I build on ideas.

- I recognize the power and grace of the Law of Attraction.

- I ask "Who can help?" And I accept it!

5

How?

Any intelligent fool can make things bigger and more complex....
It takes a touch of genius—and a lot of courage to move
in the opposite direction.

—Albert Einstein

In 2012, a client of mine in Canada identified an opportunity. What if we did a kaizen event to improve the preventive maintenance (PM) program? What if we applied Lean Six Sigma tools and techniques to this critical element of the business? The reasoning was compelling. The current program was not efficient or effective. It took too long, disrupted operations, caused unplanned delays, and was not user-friendly. Millions of dollars in equipment and parts, as well as products, service, and customers, were at risk. Skilled maintenance mechanics were spending countless hours searching for parts, some of which were not in stock. The list of reasons "why" to pursue this project was clearly convincing. The PM program needed PM. The list of reasons "why not" to pursue the project was also evaluated and easily overcome. There were very few risks to taking on this challenge—or so it seemed. A cross-functional team of experts was then assembled to participate in the effort and a team leader and sponsor were selected to champion the project. We lined up the "who" with careful thought. My role was to coach the team leader and help facilitate the project, which would soon morph into multiple kaizen events.

The question we now faced was "How?" This was a massive project encompassing hundreds of assets at multiple sites requiring monthly, semi-annual, and annual PMs. The PM process differed from one asset to another and, in some cases, took several days to complete. Spare parts ranged in the thousands and were tracked by a sophisticated software program owned and managed by another department. In many cases, the parts were not available when needed and lead times to replenish parts could take weeks. High-paid maintenance personnel were spending a considerable amount of time searching for and chasing down spare parts, often while the equipment was down and people were waiting. How were we supposed to tackle something this complex and overwhelming in a three- to five-day kaizen event? How were we supposed to eat this elephant?

W. Edwards Deming once said that hard work and best efforts without the guidance of profound knowledge might well be the root of our ruination. There is no substitute for knowledge. Our ability to execute the mission in mind is fundamental to success. It does not do any good for a parent or coach to yell at a child to swim faster if the child does not know how to swim. Yelling louder or getting angry does not help, either. In fact, it often makes things worse. I have often had this conversation with managers who think yelling and fear-based motivation are the answer.

Zentrepreneurs understand that the "how" is where the action is. Knowing what to do is often the easy part. Knowing how to do it is what makes the difference. Assuming the activity is necessary and value-added, the how is where we focus our improvement efforts. How can we do what we do better, faster, at lower cost, and in a more user-friendly way? How can we improve our overall performance? How do we turn good ideas into great results? How do we get out of the way and lead? How do we create a culture of innovation and fearlessness? How?

People all over the world have good ideas, including some that might change the world. So why is it that more people do not act on their ideas? Why is it that many organizations do not tap into these ideas quickly and effectively to improve performance and gain advantage? And why is it that among those who do, the results often come up short. It is no secret that most entrepreneurs fall short in their initial attempts at getting a business started. Is it that the idea is not valid, or is it something else? My research and experience suggest that there are significant gaps in knowing how to transform culture, eliminate fear, and turn good ideas into great results. Many people are simply not trained on how to plan the idea and execute the plan. There are scoping gaps, credibility gaps, marketing gaps, sales gaps, operations gaps, management gaps, and measurement gaps—to name a few. It is in closing these gaps that everything comes together.

The "tool belt" we use in business and operational excellence is referred to as DMAIC. This acronym stands for define, measure, analyze, improve, and control. I refer to it as a "tool belt" because there are many planning and problem-solving tools that hang off each letter. For example, in the define phase, we use voice of customer (VOC) tools such as panels, forums, and surveys to be clear on defining exactly what the customer does and does not value. We use process-mapping tools to define the current state process. We use charters to define the mission, scope, team, and expectations of the selected improvement projects. We use data collection plans to define what data we want to collect, who is going to get it, how we are going to get it, and how we want to display it. Additional tools exist for measuring, analyzing, improving, and controlling. Here are a few examples relating to DMAIC:

Define

- Voice of customer—critical to wow factors.

- Current state process—value stream maps, process maps, flow charts.

- Project charters—what, why, who, when, scope, expectations, constraints.

- Data collection plan—what, how, who, when, and how to display.

- UDEs—undesirable effects, brutal facts.

Measure

- Time—lead times, cycle times, changeover times, down time, up time.

- Quality—right-first-time yields, defects, incidents, risks.

- Cost—material, labor, rework, non-value-added activity, waste, opportunity.

- Safety—incidents, types, areas, risks, losses.

- Morale—involvement, participation, teamwork, ideas, confidence.

- Variation—times, quality, amounts, people, equipment, methods, material.

- Measurement system accuracy.

Analyze

- IPO diagram—input-output correlation, hypothesis testing.

- Pareto charts—critical few, 80/20 rule.

- Root cause—fishbone diagram, 5 Whys, weighted matrix, causal circle, reality tree.

- Design of experiment—experimental inputs to optimize outputs.

- Return on investment—P&L impact, cash flows, balance sheet, scalability.

- Risk—failure mode and effects analysis, force field analysis.

Improve

- Kaizen events.

- Design for Lean Six Sigma and manufacturability.

- Future-state mapping and implementation.

- Pilots.

Control

- Standard work—standard time, standard sequence, standard amounts, standard methods.

- Visual control—5S, color codes, scoreboards.

- Statistical process control—control charts, daily monitoring.

- Kanban—inventory management system, pull techniques, fast replenishment.

- Poka-yoke—mistake-proofing, error-proofing.

- Gemba—daily attention, manage with presence.

The value in using a rational problem-solving tool belt like DMAIC is that it helps keep teams focused and aligned as we proceed through planned change. Without this form of discipline, people can quickly become overwhelmed, jump to conclusions, give up, or fall out of line. Some people will fast forward to the improve phase with ideas about how to solve the problem without any basis in fact and analysis of the problem itself. Others might be trapped in the weeds, digging into data that doesn't matter. Still others might be idled with "analysis paralysis," overcomplicating the problem. Without a disciplined problem-solving structure, zenergy is quickly lost, because team energy is wasted on one another rather than on the mission at hand. Misalignment wears people down.

DMAIC

Control   Define

DMAIC

Improve   Measure

Analyze

DMAIC is simply a discipline that helps keep teams aligned and moving forward in a clear, compelling, and rational manner. Zentrepreneurs use it because it is smart and practical. We start by defining the mission, the scope, the expectations, the priorities, and the timing. Without this clarity, well-intentioned teams can easily get off track. We use SMART goals—specific, measureable, attainable, relevant, and timed—to articulate roles, expectations, and accountabilities. We define what data we need to collect, who will collect it, and how we will display it in the most meaningful way. We then move into the measurement phase to establish a baseline in fact and ground the team in reality. We get the brutal facts, observe behaviors, and interview people. We solicit feedback. We map the way work is done now. We uncover the UDEs (undesirable effects), and quantify them. What bothers people? Where is the waste? Where are the gaps? Where are the delays? Where are the constraints? What are the standards? Do we even have standards? Where is the variability? What is really going on? What is missing? How much? When? Is the data accurate? What do the data reveal? The devil is frequently in the details.

Data in isolation tells us very little. In fact, it is a waste of time to collect data we do not need or actually use. This brings us to the analyze phase of DMAIC. The key to this step is turning data into meaningful information, knowledge, and intelligence. Why do we have the results we have? What are the critical inputs to the measured outputs? What are the causes to the undesirable effects? What is the relationship between X and Y? In Six Sigma terminology, we call this the transfer function where $y = f(x)$. By identifying the root causes to systemic problems, or the leverage points, we can indeed make profound change. It is here that we unveil the "how of wow."

The improve phase of DMAIC is where the real action is. This is where we turn good ideas into great results. This is the essence of kaizen and zentrepreneurship. By aligning team members with a clear definition and focus, grounding them in the facts of the current state, analyzing the data together, and brainstorming solutions, we zenergize the team. We magnify and compound the energy required for positive change. We overcome the resistance that every change agent faces. We pilot our ideas, prove our hypotheses, and monitor and evaluate the results. We solicit more feedback, make necessary adjustments, and use evidence to prove the changes are better. We demonstrate "the how of wow." As Deming said, there is no substitute for knowledge. From here we move into the control phase of DMAIC, identifying and implementing the necessary controls to hold the gains.

In the preventive maintenance example, I challenged the team leader and team sponsor to re-scope the project into multiple kaizen events. We were not going to boil the ocean or solve world hunger in one event. We needed to eat the elephant one bite at a time. I suggested that we select one group of like assets and optimize the specific PM process for those assets. In this case, we scoped the first kaizen event to a particular type of press at one specific site, of which there were seven in total. This was a key asset, and the lessons and benefits could be spread quickly across all seven assets and at least one other site. We would then kaizen another group of like assets, using the lessons learned from the first kaizen event. We now had a more manageable scope and a much less daunting mission to complete. We clarified the how.

Confidence and morale increased almost immediately. We also used the define phase of DMAIC to clarify timing and expectations. The plan was to have a prototype design for a PM "kitting" structure so that the mechanics always had exactly what they needed for the job when they needed it. This included creating the actual kits, locating them in a standard location, defining the standard number of kits to be ready at any given time, defining the rules of engagement, defining a standard replenishment process to ensure readiness, defining a sustainability plan, and being ready to pilot the new system within five days. This clarity of focus and practicality was of enormous help to a team that was originally thinking they had to tackle the entire asset management program, including all of the required software changes to go with it. In this case, the prototypes we witnessed on Thursday of the kaizen event did not require any changes to software or purchasing policies. The real awakening was simply that, as of that Thursday, there were only enough parts available to make one or two kits when several more were needed. This reinforced the need for this project and breathed more life into the team. No wonder the maintenance program looked as if it were thrashing about in the water about to drown; it didn't know how to swim! The team now knew we were successful with this first PM kaizen event, and we were motivated to apply the "how" to many more. This first bite of the elephant tasted good.

It takes more than a few quick wins to sustain change. Aristotle once said, "We are what we repeatedly do. Excellence, then, is not an act but a habit."[1] This brings us to the control phase of DMAIC. Many good ideas fall from grace, not because they are not valid, but because people are creatures of habit. It often takes time and repetition to form new habits. We need to be patient with this part of the change process. The control phase offers tools such as standard work routines, standard times, standard metrics, standard monitoring, statistical process control, visual scoreboards, daily "huddles," and other tactics to guide and form new habits. The zentrepreneur understands that change can be disruptive and many people prefer the certainty of what they are already doing over the uncertainty of something new—even if the new approach is better!

Most of the good ideas that have come my way through the years required learning on my part. In other words, I did not know how to execute the ideas, and this presented a major obstacle for me. I would often contemplate the questions what if, why, why not, and who, but I was sometimes stumped by how to turn these visions into reality. They just seemed like dreams—impractical and unrealistic. How do we accomplish things that seem impossible?

I suppose Thomas Edison, the Wright brothers, Henry Ford, and many other zentrepreneurs have wondered the same thing? How do we do the "how"? Without clarity on how to manifest good ideas into great results, they go nowhere. We have to move beyond the dream to the practical steps necessary to manifest the dream. We have to clearly define what it is we want to accomplish. We have to set SMART goals. We have to get the facts and establish an accurate baseline. We have to use competent analysis to turn data into information and information into knowledge. We then have to turn the knowledge into innovation and the innovation into results by applying bold initiative, action, and perseverance. These steps apply to ideas in any arena. Here is a sampling of some of the professional business experiences to which I have learned to apply zentrepreneurship. In each case, I had to learn how to manifest the idea into reality:

- Leading corporate culture change in multiple industries.

- Aligning senior management teams in many countries.

- Implementing high-performance work teams.

- Leaning waste out of an organization.

- Negotiating win-win labor contracts.

- Wowing customers.

- Starting new businesses.

- Designing training materials and simulations.

- Conducting workshops and seminars worldwide.

- Coaching executives and managers.

- Resolving conflicts.

- Improving methods, processes, and procedures.

- Inspiring people by transcending ego, fear, and doubt.

- Improving financial performance.

- Writing award-winning and best-selling books.

- Marketing and reaching people worldwide.

Remember: most of the good ideas that come our way require learning on *our* part! Here is one specific example. In 1993, my older brother gave me an idea. He suggested I write an allegory. He had just read my first book, *Pulling Together*, and he liked the stories I told to reinforce the points I was trying to make. He said I had an interesting way of explaining the theory using easy-to-understand, practical examples. What if I wrote an allegory? I listened and then I said, "Sounds good. What is an allegory?" He answered my question and then urged me to read a few examples to learn more. He even loaned me one. I followed his advice, seeking to learn how to write such a story, and followed with my second book, *Agent of Change: Leading a Cultural Revolution.* Evidently, this was a good idea, because this book got the attention of several very credible leaders, who endorsed it with positive recommendations. Military leaders, CEOs, best-selling authors, the U.S. Ambassador to Italy, and a multi-billionaire all offered positive comments. All I had to do was take a good idea, learn how to do it, and get it done. Such is the way of the zentrepreneur.

In this age of information and innovation, we all have the capacity to learn more. If there is something we do not know how to do, there are plenty of resources available to explore it further. We can learn to lead, manage, sell, speak, learn, teach, listen, and write more effectively. If the desire and passion are there, coupled with an open and inquisitive mind, there is no end to what we can learn. The zentrepreneur gets this. Life is all about expansion, relationships, and growth. Individually and corporately, if we are not growing, we are dying.

The challenge of how is often what intrigues the zentrepreneur. It is like solving an interesting riddle or puzzle. It taps the creative potential we all have. If the reason is compelling enough, it is frequently our own self-doubt and fear that are most obstructive. Somewhere in the equation, we have to build a little confidence, courage, momentum, and faith, something I meditate on every day. We have to build a team. We have to build a constituency for change. We have to cultivate a collective mind. In many cases, I have been utterly surprised by what I find.

One example of this took place with a kaizen event I facilitated in Portugal in 2007. This particular event was challenging and memorable. To keep this facility open and preserve hundreds of jobs, the team had to find a way to run a seven-day continuous operation in five days per week without any capital expenditure. We had five days to figure it out.

When I arrived, the team was assembled but clearly concerned. Some people were in a state of complete disbelief. How were we going to come up with that much "free capacity"? The operation was already running a 24/7 schedule, and there was no idle equipment—or so the team thought. We set to work following the DMAIC methodology. We gathered facts, prepared process maps, crunched numbers, analyzed data, developed alternatives, tested hypotheses, and drew conclusions—all reinforcing what some team members seemed to expect all along. The mission appeared to be impossible. The plant was destined to close. It was Monday afternoon and people were feeling anguished, so we decided to take a walk. We started on the factory floor, investigating every piece of equipment involved. The primary constraint operation was obvious, a specific type of chemical reactor. There was no doubt about it. To achieve a five-day schedule, the team needed to come up with an additional reactor—fast!

Another constraint was the absence of capital. There was no money in the budget to purchase additional equipment, and these reactors were very expensive. We pressed on searching for hidden capacity within existing reactors, but no such capacity could be found. The team turned to me for help and guidance. There had to be light somewhere in this tunnel. A hunch told me to keep looking. I asked to see their warehouse. This seemingly odd request was met with a blend of blank stares and raised eyebrows. What could we possibly find in the warehouse that might solve this problem? The warehouse is mostly full of spare parts and junk. Ten minutes later, expressions changed from hopeless disbelief to astonished disbelief. There in front of us was the exact chemical reactor we needed, still in a crate and never before used. We were back in the game. No one was quite sure where the reactor came from or how it got there, but it was there. Once again, I witnessed what many would call a miracle. We had what we needed to move forward, and it wasn't just the reactor. We had a change of mind. By Friday, we had a plan in place to keep the facility open and the necessary changes were already underway. This meant clearing several other hurdles and secondary constraints, but these tasks seemed effortless once we had some momentum. This is what is referred to in the Tao as *wu wei* or "effortless manifestation." The zentrepreneur cherishes this powerful and graceful flow. The zentrepreneur believes in miracles.

I enjoy facilitating kaizen events for this very reason. It is a wonderful way to teach people how to experience different results by altering perception. I remember one event in Michigan where our mission was to take a 19-hour process down to four hours within five days. To make the mission even more challenging, this particular process had a range of 15 hours to 29 hours, meaning that no one ever knew how long the process was actually going to take. This variation in time and performance made it especially difficult for the people in the planning and scheduling departments, not to mention the people directly involved in the process.

We kicked off the session on Monday morning by reviewing the project charter with the team, including the four-hour goal by Thursday. By mid-morning break on the first day, one of the senior team members approached me with serious concerns. He explained that several other team members had expressed extreme doubt about our mission. Through their eyes, the idea of a four-hour goal was ludicrous, especially because the last sample we reviewed took 27 hours. How were we supposed to take a process that long and complex, and complete it within four hours by Thursday? Perfect, I thought to myself. We have an opportunity to change minds, not just the process in focus. I shared my optimism with the senior team member, who shrugged his shoulders and wandered off shaking his head. I get this initial reaction a lot.

When the team reconvened, there was little doubt about the doubt. It reminded me of a group of people feeling lost in the dark without any sense of direction. Someone needed to turn on a light and point the way to the door. Otherwise, it was utter confusion and chaos. By Tuesday afternoon, after breaking through many limiting beliefs, memes, and mental barriers, we found a light switch. Then we found a door, giving us a way out. This was followed by hope. Next, we began charting a course to turn hope into promise and promise into conviction. By Wednesday afternoon, we had a detailed plan of action, and we were preparing for a "test flight" on Thursday. More importantly, we had a team of people who had gone from complete skepticism and doubt on Monday, to high expectations and enthusiasm by Wednesday.

The pilot on Thursday took four hours and 20 minutes. Given the dramatic improvement, one might now have thought that the new process design was a spectacular success. In fact, the executive vice president for this multi-billion dollar company visited the pilot demonstration and expressed his elation with the team and their spirited progress. The improvement was worth millions of dollars in freed-up capacity and a vast improvement in working conditions. This helped, but the team was now disappointed in missing their target. I found myself laughing. Here was a team that on Monday couldn't imagine doing the process in less than 15 hours, and now they are kicking themselves for accomplishing it in just over four hours.

We have all experienced some degree of doubt in our lives. It is human. It is an element of the ego thought system, and we all have conditioning and challenges with this subconscious thought system. It is not always easy to let go. Indeed, when people get stressed, there is a tendency to hold on tighter, to cling to the very anchor dragging us under. Learning how to identify, confront, and overcome doubt is essential to leading change successfully. The more we practice this, the better we get at it.

When I started my consulting business in 1988, I had very little knowledge of how to build a successful practice. I had ideas. I had a vision. I had a variety of business and management experiences that would help. I had every intention of stepping up and doing it right. But I had not yet done it. I did not know what I did not know.

In a word, I was ignorant. This would be a limiting factor. This would be my greatest competition. What could I do about my own ignorance?

Recognizing this gap in my plan, I set out to learn everything I could from wise and trusted experts. I listened to consultants who had been there, done that. I read books on the subject from credible and competent authorities. I surrounded myself with experienced professionals and asked for honest and candid feedback on my ideas and performance. Several of my books are actually suggestions from some of these wise and trusted allies. I also challenged much of the advice I was offered from questionable sources. There was certainly plenty of that—including a list of things I would never be able to do effectively, like write professionally or be published!

Of course, learning how requires more than theoretical, book knowledge. Confucius once said, "What I hear, I forget. What I see, I remember. What I do, I understand." This means we have to apply the knowledge in order to really get it. For example, we can study golf. We can learn the rules about golf. We can watch videos and read magazines about golf. We can be trained on the etiquette. We can memorize all of the clubs and when to use each club. But until we actually try hitting that little white ball, we do not really get golf. On the contrary, we might learn quickly that we have a lot to learn. Reality can be quite humbling from time to time.

Many professionals refer to their work as a practice: people practice medicine, law, and yoga and meditation. The zentrepreneur practices turning good ideas into great results. The zentrepreneur practices innovation and fearlessness. The zentrepreneur practices letting go and getting out of the way. There is no end to this journey. There is no point of perfection. It is ongoing and continuous, a lifelong learning. Fear and doubt are limiting factors. The insecure ego holds us back. Ideas must pass through a threshold of uncertainty to be tested and realized. We have to step up to the plate to get a hit. We have to cross the bridge of courage to reach the field of enlightenment and true prosperity. Stop and think about some of the good ideas that have come your way. What happened to them? Where are they now?

I have let go of many ideas over the years. The reason for me is simple: they did not elicit enough passion for me to pursue them further. I dabbled in real estate for a period of time, learning how along the way. I invested time and money in the financial markets, actively trading for several years. I took a stab at writing children's books and drawing cartoons for a year or two. I tried my hand at career counseling. I spent time in a corporate setting as an analyst, manager, and director. These were all good ideas, but ultimately my heart and passion took me in a different direction. To me, this is essential to success. Our work must be our play. Our passion must be aligned with our purpose. We all have a calling and we know it when we make the connection. We know it when we feel it.

Zentrepreneurs are willing to make great sacrifices to see a vision through. We see it as part of the journey, an experience of lifelong learning and continuous training. We learn how by learning how. It is difficult to do this if our hearts and souls are not aligned with our mission. True passion is not something we can fake. Integrity cannot be manipulated. We chase our purpose and get our paychecks to chase us. Many people have this equation backward, chasing paychecks throughout life rather than purpose. We tend to execute with the skills of a master because we clear a lot of the subconscious baggage off our plates. The zentrepreneur has nothing to prove. The letting-go process has lightened the load of the egotistical need for approval, pride, security, and control. This is the field that the great mystic Rumi spoke of when he wrote, "There is a field beyond right and wrong. I will meet you there." It is here that we find equanimity, grace, and peace of mind.

Checklist for Success

- I know the difference between "I think" and "I know."

- I recognize that the "how" is where the action is.

- I use a rational, disciplined model such as DMAIC to solve problems and lead change.

- I am self-directed and proactive in searching for answers.

- I set SMART goals to clarify expectations and get things done.

- I let go of ideas and constraints holding me back.

- I chase my purpose rather than my paycheck.

- My purpose and passion are aligned.

- I am willing to make sacrifices to get results.

- I continue to practice every day.

- I ask "How?" and learn how—as fast as I can!

6

When?

If we all did the things we are capable of doing,
we would literally astound ourselves.

—Thomas Edison

In November 2009, I was invited to meet with an executive from a former client. He had changed jobs since I last worked for him, and he was now a senior vice president for a global manufacturing and supply company. He contacted our team because he was interested in bringing in someone he trusted to help accelerate the Continuous Improvement and Operational Excellence efforts he had underway at two of his sites. The CI efforts had commenced about a year earlier under the direction and guidance of a well-known consulting firm with a team of trained "Black Belts" in Lean Six Sigma. Unfortunately, there was an absence of measureable results. There was a lot of activity, but very little productivity. The executive now in charge knew from prior experience that we could move things along quickly and effectively, and he wanted results sooner, not later. Therefore, like a true zentrepreneur, he exercised the what if, why, why not, the who, and the how with his executive team, and we were given the go-ahead to engage. It was now all about the "when."

Time is one of the most common excuses I hear people use to not do something that is valuable and important, or to take longer than need be. Think about this and contemplate the same questions. How often do you hear people say they need more time? How often do you say this? How often do you hear people say they do not have time to read, exercise, sleep, spend time with family and friends, or accomplish more? How often are people late for meetings? How often do meetings run longer than they should? How often are suppliers late or short with service or deliveries? How often are people delayed in responding to your calls, e-mails, or needs? How can it take some companies weeks or months to do a few hours of value-added activity? On countless occasions, I have observed organizations taking more than 180 days to do three to five days of value-added activity. In fact, it is quite common to find that the percentage of value-added time from total time is only about 0.5 to 5 percent. This means that more than 95 percent of the time a material or product is "in play" in the value stream, nothing of value is happening to it. It is simply waiting, or being inspected, or being transported, or being tested. This is like waiting an hour for a 30-second ride at the amusement park.

We all have 24 hours in a day. How is it that some people and organizations get so much more accomplished in the same amount of time than others? Zentreprenuers understand that time is money. It matters to customers, patients, passengers, researchers, designers, innovators, builders, team members, and supply chains. It matters to anyone seriously interested in being healthy and successful. Therefore, we have to find ways to optimize our use of time from a multitude of perspectives. In fact, time is now one of the most critical success factors among enlightened purchasing agents, right up there with quality, service, price, and efficacy. Buyers will frequently purchase products and services from vendors if it will save them time, solve problems quickly, turn inventories faster, reduce waste, and accelerate cash flow. Think about this the next time you buy a product from Amazon or Wal-Mart. One of the reasons why the product is priced so competitively is because savings are being passed on to you, the consumer. Some of these savings come from good inventory and cash management practices. In all likelihood, you are giving Amazon and Wal-Mart your cash for a product they have not yet had to pay for. This is not because they pay their bills late. On the contrary, it is because the inventories turn so fast that the bill for what you bought is not yet due. This is a form of time-based management, a powerful business strategy used by many world-class businesses today to create competitive advantages, improve cash flow, and provide more value to end-users. Innovators worldwide use similar time strategies to "get there first," often resulting in market dominance until others catch up. Put another way, the first one to get the new idea to market wins! Zentrepreneurs and enlightened managers get this!

When we begin to see time as an ally and a critical success factor rather than an excuse, we awaken the zentrepreneurial mindset. We see the bigger picture. We get more in tune with the overall system and flow. The question "when?" is simply a reminder that time matters. It is a form of discipline. It sharpens our focus. It is specific, measureable, and relevant. It helps establish accountability. To turn good ideas into great results, we have to pay attention to time. To create a culture of innovation and fearlessness, we have to start now. Now is the only time there ever really is. The world will not stop turning to wait for us. We have to act on our ideas, and we have to use time wisely. Use these questions to focus your efforts:

- When are we going to start?

- When are we going to finish?

- What is our total cycle time?

- How much of the total cycle time is actually value-added time?

- Where are we wasting time?

- What activities can we eliminate?

- When will we meet and for how long? Is this our best use of time?

- How will we manage our time when we do meet?

- What time-based metrics will we use to measure performance?

- What would it take to accomplish the mission successfully in less time?

The executive I started working with in late 2009 had something every zentrepreneur has: a sense of urgency. We got started working with the CI team and quickly learned that the Black Belts and project leaders had been programmed to believe that their projects should take six to 12 months. What a revelation!

Using many of the zentrepreneurial strategies and tools highlighted in this book, we set to work with this new client. We pulled the Black Belts together and trained them in baseline analysis. We defined, measured, and analyzed a key value stream, using data rather than opinion to tell the story. We identified several strategic projects using systems-thinking and cross-functional analysis. We scoped and staffed the projects effectively to get some quick results and build momentum. Within four months, the teams had millions of dollars in annualized improvements to show for their efforts. In fact, several executives from this global company's international sites came to benchmark the activity and bring the lessons back to their own sites. Time is money. The message here was clear: Stop making excuses. Get out of the way and lead!

In 2001, I got another call. This one was from the CEO of a multi-billion-dollar company based in Michigan. I happened to be working in Philadelphia at the time, but I remember the call well. I was on the way to the airport when the phone rang. The man introduced himself and asked if I would be willing to come in and talk with members of his executive team about Lean Six Sigma and culture change. I agreed and the meeting was scheduled. When I arrived at the company's headquarters a few weeks later, I was shown to the executive boardroom, where about 15 people awaited me. I was not aware that I would be meeting with so many people. The CEO had originally asked if I would simply come in and speak with him and a few others.

The energy in the room was anything but zenergy. There was an aura of fear, doubt, and skepticism present.

The feeling was tense, distrusting, and defensive. The ego thought system was lurking about like a sly serpent beneath the massive conference table, tempting the executive team to play it safe and protect themselves. Who is this change agent coming in here anyway? What does he know that we don't know? I found it almost amusing. First, I had no stake in the game. I was simply invited to come in and share my insights on some global best practices. A member of this company's board of directors and a former CEO had become familiar with my work and encouraged the existing CEO to contact me. I had no slides or handouts to offer. I had no speech prepared. It was simply me and a rather large team of skeptics. I actually run into this more often than not. There is no level of any organizational chart that is immune to fear and insecurity. In fact, the higher some people climb in the ranks, the more protective, defensive, and risk-averse they become. It is as if they shift into defense mode, protecting their own status quo. Why should we do this? Why should we do it now? How will this affect me?

I shared a few insights and drew a few pictures on a flipchart. I did what any zentrepreneur would do: I spoke with heart, enthusiasm, and positive intent. I used rhetorical questions to create intrigue and stimulate thinking. I invited pushback and healthy dialogue. I used facts and data to support my observations, and shared specific examples to give context to the content. I explained the most common reasons why many cultural change efforts fail in organizations and what can be done up-front to avoid these predictable failure modes. From our research, we know that the top two reasons for failure with this kind of initiative are leadership misalignment and the absence of genuine management support and commitment. In most cases, these two failure modes go together. Senior management doesn't really understand what they are signing up for, and the rest of the management team gets in the way due to confusion, ignorance, fear, and flawed assumptions.

Our countermeasures for these two failure modes are comprehensive leadership education on the topic and the baseline analysis process, which builds top management focus, understanding, alignment, and support. In fact, we conclude the baseline analysis week with a "Contract for Change," a simple document that specifies that all parties agree to support the projects identified. This is not a legal document. It is more symbolic in nature, serving as a reminder that we all understand the content and context of the projects, and we agree to support them with our time, attention, and resources.

When the meeting was over, the CEO walked me out and thanked me. He said what I did was spot on and just exactly what he was looking for—nothing formal, no song and dance, just genuine, authentic, and credible.

Evidently, he simply wanted to start the conversation with his leadership team to see how they would respond and where it would go. He was looking for a credible resource to spark that conversation. They were still a long way from making any kind of commitment to get out of the way and lead. Put another way, there was no sense of urgency, no zentrepreneurial spirit, no enthusiasm to step up. The senior leadership team was clearly the primary constraint and leverage point, which is often the case. Great teams require great coaching. I continued to follow up and stay in contact, but apparently it takes some executive teams a while to decide to adopt global best practices. This reminds me of an old riddle: Five frogs are on a log. One decides to jump off. How many are left? The answer is five, because deciding is not the same as doing. We have to act on our ideas to see results quickly.

Two years later, I was asked if I would come back and meet with the executive team again. The zentrepreneur in me said yes, of course. Why not? I might learn something. I might be able to help. There might be great potential and opportunity here. Perhaps it is just a matter of time. In some ways, it is always a matter of time. Sooner or later, we learn our lessons, one way or another.

The overall team was still hesitant and somewhat resistant to jump into a major corporate cultural initiative with both feet, so it was decided that we would test the water with a pilot at one of their sites. If it worked there, we could scale it up to other sites in the United States and Mexico. I accepted the assignment, and within six months, the results were already telling a very compelling story. A site that was close to being sold or shut down was now quickly on the rebound. A new culture of innovation and fearlessness was coming forth as the systems and structure were optimized for flow and peak performance. Put good people on a winning team, and it will not be long before they start believing they can win. We are all creatures of habit. Healthy habits lead to healthy results

Within the next 18 months, we deployed the same cultural transformation at sites in Michigan, New York, and Mexico. To this day, I am very thankful for being able to help this organization, a publicly held company whose value has more than quintupled since its transformation. Despite one of the worst recessions in the past century, this company continues to use these best practices to grow and prosper at a stellar rate. I just wonder why it took so long to get started and at what opportunity cost. Did this company even consider the cost of doing nothing (CODN)? What were they really afraid of? Time is on our side when we use it wisely.

A few years ago, I was asked to return to this company to walk through and share my observations. What I observed that day was magnificent. The managers and teams I had trained years earlier went on to train others and deliver benchmark results that they were very proud of. It was a sight to see. A teacher had taught them to fish, and they were now reeling in prize catches while teaching others to fish. The students were now the teachers, and the constituency for change was growing. A culture of innovation and fearlessness was unfolding.

Zentrepreneurs have a keen sense of time and the use of time. We know that it is a valuable resource and we must use it wisely. We must prioritize our activities and delete any distractions that interfere with effective time management. In today's world, it is so easy to be distracted by electronics, smartphones, e-mails, meetings, interruptions, dependencies, unhealthy habits, and bureaucratic, non-value-added activity. The irony is that many of the new technologies that we expect to help save us time actually eat up a lot of our time if we are not aware and discerning. How many apps do we really need on our phone? Is our smartphone tempting us to do dumb things? How much time do we really need to spend on social media? How sophisticated does our software need to be to track and report simple things? Do we really need to e-mail someone who is sitting across the aisle from us? Are we complicating the simple or simplifying the complex?

A few years ago, I was asked to coach an executive in New York. The firm he worked for valued him as a long-time employee but had concerns about his micro-management style. I paid him a visit, and we started with an assessment that included defining and measuring his typical day. (This is an example of how the DMAIC methodology can be used for improving personal performance as well as corporate performance.) We started with define and measure. What exactly was he doing? How was he spending his time? How did he see his role? What value was he providing in the time he had? How did he know how he was doing? What metrics was he using to assess performance? What were his boss's perceptions? What were his peers' perceptions? What were his employees' perceptions? What were his perceptions? Was there any "perception warp," a term I like to use to describe the common disconnect many people have with the people they work with. Perception warp is a hidden cause to many unhealthy relationships—at work and at home.

As it turned out, he spent a significant amount of time on e-mails and interruptions. He was caught up in a "dependency syndrome." This means that whenever an employee had a problem, they delegated it up to the boss. He was his own constraint. Micro-managers and controlling personality types often bring this on themselves. So do entrepreneurs and small business owners at some level. Rather than teach responsibility, they take it away. Rather than enable and empower people, they disable and demotivate them. Rather than getting out of the way and leading, they get in the way and slow things down. This is a classic sign of insecurity, fear, and weakness. We mean well, but we struggle with letting go. We care, but ironically and paradoxically, we are careless. To create a culture of innovation and fearlessness, we have to get out of the way and lead. We have to let go to let flow.

My client was not aware that he was spending this much time on unnecessary activity. In fact, he had come to believe that it was necessary. His perception was that his employees needed his help. People were relying on him for data, information, direction, and guidance. This perception made him feel valued and important, necessary and secure. He spent hours every day putting out fires, unaware that he could prevent them. In some cases, he was subconsciously responsible for starting them.

Wise leaders and zentrepreneurs delegate effectively. We understand the theory of constraints and we recognize that, if we are not leveraging ourselves with others, we are causing our own problems. We are the bottleneck. We are getting in the way! Using Pareto analysis, we identified the top time-wasters for my client, and then we applied what I call "Pareto the Pareto." Dig deeper to learn more about the current state. Categorize the e-mails by type, person, and reason. Do the same thing with the interruptions. Why am I being interrupted? What is the reason? Who is interrupting me and with what frequency?

Why do people need me? What is it they want? Where is
the gap? What alternatives exist? What if we try one of
these alternatives? What will happen? What is the risk?
Why not explore other ways for employees to get this information or direction? Who can I pull together to help
me solve this problem? How can we free up more time
for everyone?

Vicious circles are everywhere, and they cause per-
petual suffering. For example, if we are not organized,
we misplace things. When we need them and cannot find
them, we waste time searching for them and perhaps even
buy more things to replace them, feeding the disorgani-
zation. This cycle continues, sucking valuable time and
energy out of the day until the sage leader identifies and
eliminates the root cause. Go back and look for this on
the Causal Circle on page 42. When we fail to prevent
problems, we have more problems to solve. When we
have more problems to solve in a finite period of time, we
suffer from the illusion that we need more time. We feel
pressured and stressed. We think we need more when in
fact we should work with less. We feed our own demise.

In the case of this client, we identified some very practical and proactive options to eliminate the need for most
of the reactive e-mails and interruptions. We shifted our
time and attention to the critical inputs rather than the
lagging outputs. By implementing practices like brief,

daily "huddles," visual project management tools, and scoreboards, people could now do their work more efficiently and effectively without having to depend on the boss throughout the day. The direction for the day, the week, and the month was clear. The goals, expectations, and standards were clear. Ownership and accountability was clear. The score was clear. No longer did the athlete have to run over to the sidelines to ask the coach if the team was winning or losing, or how much time was left on the clock.

I am often asked how I seem to juggle so much at once without appearing stressed. Like many people, I am frequently asked to be in several places at once with tight deadlines in between. How is it possible to operate in these conditions without aging quickly? There are several critical inputs to these outputs—secrets to success, so to speak. To achieve higher productivity with less stress, we have to learn to think and behave differently. We have to break subconscious, conditioned habits. Stress is of the mind. If we are not mindful of it and skilled at letting it go, it will manifest into stress in the body. Dis-ease is a common root cause for disease. Fear and anxiety are contagious. Stress and doubt will transmit to others if we are not careful. An anxious and stressed leader can bring anxiety and stress to an entire team. Put simply, the disease can spread. The good news is that the same is true for the opposite situation. When a light enters a dark room, the darkness vanishes. When an enlightened zentrepreneur enters the room, people feel a difference. It is often quite subtle at first, but the zenergy is there. Now it is just a question of people opening up and allowing it to displace the doubt, resistance, and darkness.

We are all bombarded by thoughts and ideas through-out the day. Some we allow to nest in the mind, and others we quickly disregard. The thoughts we allow to nest become beliefs. Think of these like "programs" of the mind, or memes. In time, they become our habits, our autopilot. Some of these programs are helpful and others are destructive, like viruses. Our habits are run by our subconscious mind, also known as our habitual mind. These habits govern most of our lives while our conscious mind tends to one thing at a time. The subconscious mind, which is scientifically measured at more than one million times more powerful than the conscious mind, lives only in the present. It has no capacity to think in the past or the future. It tends only to the now. It monitors your heart, your blood sugar, your immediate task at hand (such as driving a car), your adrenaline, your digestive system, your patience, your reactions, your tendencies, and thousands of other concurrent activities. However, because it is subconscious, we are often not aware of the programs it runs on. This is often why "will power" fails to bring about the habit change we seek. When the conscious will meets the subconscious habit, the conditioned habit pushes back.

The conscious mind spends little time in the present. While we are on autopilot with the subconscious mind at the wheel, the conscious mind is often jumping from the past to the future and back again. This triggers stress. It is only in the future that anxiety, fear, and stress reside and it is only in the past that regret, grief, and guilt reside. Therefore, when we are not mindful of the present, the eternal and sacred now, we set ourselves up for disempowering feelings. We consciously miss the only moment that matters. Great athletes understand this, as do zentrepreneurs. When we step up to the free throw line or the golf ball, we have to pay attention to the now. We have to be in the zone. We have to be mindful of what we are doing. The past is behind us and the future is uncertain. We have to tend to the moment. Understanding this vital input is critical to letting go of stress, despite our circumstances. Fear and stress are all entangled around a future that may never come. With uncertainty comes assumption. We can assume the better or the worse. In either case, the body will respond to what the mind holds to be true. If we think the villain with the gun will pull the trigger, we will be afraid and attract stressful energy. If we think otherwise, we will behave with more poise, composure, equanimity, and confidence. The zentrepreneur understands that stress is manufactured by the mind. It is not something someone else does to us. It is something we allow. It exists either way. It is an energetic frequency, like a radio wave. We can tune in or tune out. The choice is up to us.

Another secret to achieving high productivity with low stress is in understanding the counterintuitive world of paradox. Jesus, Lao Tzu, and the Buddha were all masterful in teaching us how to accomplish more with less. For many people, the idea of going slower to move faster makes no sense. Having more by giving it all away seems illogical, imbalanced, and nonsensical. Working fewer hours sounds lazy and unprofessional, despite the results. Letting go to let flow appears weak. What about working hard? What about working long hours? What about ambition and competition? What about economics? What about supply and demand?

Zentrepreneurs are very keen on the pressures of economics, competition, and return on investment. After all, the zentrepreneur is a form of entrepreneur with very positive results. The secret here is in understanding the difference between scarcity consciousness and abundance consciousness. One with scarcity consciousness believes in shortages and lack: We lack time, space, and resources. There is only so much to go around. In order to win, someone has to lose. This ego-driven, dualistic mindset drives feelings and habits of greed, distrust, lust, possessiveness, jealousy, pride, and control. We have to stake our claim now. We have to fight to survive. We have to be tough. We have to work hard and be demanding.

The alternative to scarcity consciousness is abundance consciousness, a belief system adopted by the zentrepreneur. When we understand that the more we give the more we receive, it is easier to let go of the false attachments that we cling to. The more we teach responsibility, the more responsibility we receive. The more we do to eliminate or delegate our work, the sooner we get promoted. The more support we give, the more support we get. The more kindness we give, the friendlier people are with us. The more ideas we offer, the more creative we become. The more we are at peace, the more peace reveals itself. There is no shortage of the things that matter most.

People sometimes ask me where my ideas come from. They perceive me as creative and resourceful. My answer sometimes surprises them. I simply tell the people who ask that the ideas are not mine. They come through me, but not from me. I do not believe I generate the ideas, even though the ego would have me think otherwise and want some kind of credit for them. I allow them to flow to and through me. I attract them and then share them. It is as if they are in the air, and I am simply a receptor for them. Using the Law of Attraction, positive intent, and high-frequency zenergy, I use this effortless process to accomplish a great deal, as if I am at play. I do not use an academic degree or job title to try to convince people to take me seriously. I use zenergy.

In 2009, I was on a two-week assignment in Europe, and I had a weekend to use at my discretion. Normally when I have a time available like this, I explore the city, the cathedrals, the museums, and the culture. However, on this Saturday morning, I was given a very powerful spiritual message during my meditation. It was perfectly clear. I was directed to start writing again. It had been nearly 10 years since I wrote my last book, and I no longer felt the passion. My father died in 2000, and I just seemed to lose interest in writing after that. Couple that feeling with a very busy consulting and speaking schedule, and I simply felt no compelling reason to return to the practice. True to high-frequency zenergy, this message would not go away. It was as if some sacred force was in the room with me insisting I pay attention. The "what if" was given to me. What if I write a spiritual book about helping people find more inner peace? The "why" was also given to me—or so I thought. Initially, the reasons included helping people learn ways to let go of fear, doubt, and disbelief. Plenty of people could benefit from that, including me. The "why not" was the biggest challenge for me at the time. Why not write this book? There were plenty of reasons: I had very little time available to commit to it. My schedule was full for the next four months. I had never written a spiritual book before. All of my prior books were of the business and self-help genres. I didn't even know what to say. Then the "who" became clear to me. I would not be writing this book alone. In fact, it was a humble reminder that I had spiritual help with all of my prior work but just didn't fully realize it. Suddenly, the words of St. Francis were crystal clear: "Make me an instrument of your peace." Now I have to laugh. I started writing that day without any clear idea of where I was going. Zentrepreneurs do have faith.

I wrote all day Saturday and Sunday that weekend, channeling the flowing ideas into words. My biggest concerns now were how and when I would finish this book and who would publish it. When I returned home a week later, I learned that all of my consulting work for the next four months was either rescheduled or cancelled. We were in the midst of a major recession, and companies worldwide were cutting back on consultants and training. I now had four months of open space on my calendar. Go figure!

Normally, this kind of synchronicity might have frightened me. Why me? Why now? What did I do to deserve this? How was I going to get through this? How was I going to pay the bills? The recession had already cost me a small fortune. Then the words I was writing into this new book calmed me. The "Ring of Peace," a four-step model, guided me through what was one of the most tumultuous years in my life, with a sense of equanimity, inner peace, and grace. I learned to let be, let go, let see, and let flow. The writing of the book was for me! What a revelation! And it was for anyone else like me going through turbulent times. Little did I know at the time that in less than a year my situation would get even worse. The cutback in work and financial crisis was enough to stress most people. Add to that an upcoming divorce and the loss of a loved one, and the book could not have come at a better time. It was as if I was being given a spiritual heads up.

I worked on that book diligently for the next four months and when I finally finished the first draft, all of my consulting work picked back up. The book was subsequently published and then awarded the Editor's Choice "Best Inspirational Book of 2010" by Allbooks Review in Toronto. More importantly, the process of writing that book opened my heart, mind, and eyes to profound spiritual lessons I had no conscious knowledge of. It was as if I was awakened to a whole new mystical playing field, a deeper awareness of who and what I really am. Now there is no going back. A butterfly cannot return to a caterpillar.

Blaise Pascal once wrote, "The heart has reasons that reason cannot know." The challenge many intellectuals have is in listening to the heart. Is it any coincidence that heart disease is one of the most prominent forms of suffering in the United States? Is this really just about what we eat and drink and do for exercise? Does a chemical pill really have any effect on the root cause? What would the world be like if we paid more attention to this conduit of sacred energy? What would corporate culture be like in terms of innovation and fearlessness if we put more heart into our work?

There is always time to do what matters most. Logic and intellect may disagree and perhaps even trap us in the paradigm of scarcity. Zentrepreneurs challenge this paradigm. We think outside this box. We know that there is no lack of anything truly important. There is only imbalance. There are only denial and resistance that creates the illusion of scarcity. When we understand that time itself is an illusion and that, from a spiritual perspective, the only time is now, we can act with more poise and grace. We can align ourselves with the Tao, the great current of life. We can get things done more effectively in less time. We can accomplish more with less effort. We can bring light into the darkness of despair and doubt. Now is always our one and only chance to be the change we want to see in the world, as Gandhi so eloquently put it many years ago.

Checklist for Success

- I believe there is plenty of time to do what matters most.

- I use time to my advantage.

- I use time to set priorities and focus efforts.

- I recognize that there is a critical difference between deciding and doing.

- I consider the opportunity costs of doing nothing or procrastinating.

- I challenge the "adding" paradigm by finding things to subtract.

- I eliminate time-wasting activity.

- I delete viruses of the mind, subconscious programs that interfere with success.

- I believe in abundance, not scarcity.

- I am mindful of the present, the sacred and eternal now.

- I define, measure, and analyze how I use my time.

- I find and break vicious circles in my life and in my business.

- I use paradoxical questions to generate creative, counterintuitive alternatives.

- I challenge the amount of time it really takes to get things done.

- I ask "when" to clarify expectations and establish accountability.

7

Yeah, But...

A book on leading change would not be complete without a chapter on resistance. Change agents meet resistance every day. I like to call it the "yeah, buts." We all run into this. We express a good idea, provide our analysis, offer a solution, share our rationale, and propose a plan. And we are met with a host of reasons why the idea won't work: "This isn't a good time. We can't afford it. We don't have the skill or the capability or the capacity. We're already doing it. We're working on it. Other stakeholders won't buy into it. We have too many other priorities." The list goes on and on.

Zentrepreneurs expect resistance. The difference is in how we handle it. Unlike many people, we do not fight it or resist it head on with force, for this only makes it stronger. There are alternatives to using force. Instead, we plan on it. We actually look for ways to use the resistance to our advantage. Maybe there is good reason for the "yeah, but." Perhaps we missed this in our Force Field Analysis or our Failure Mode and Effects Analysis. It might be wise to listen carefully. It might be prudent on our part to ensure balance in the equation. Perhaps we can use the resistance to gain more insight, knowledge, and credibility. This reaction simply brings us back to the why and why not questions we covered earlier.

In 2008, I was asked to lead a major continuous improvement effort at a facility in France. This facility was one of many for a large U.S.–based company, and it was the top performer in the corporation. For this reason, the site director pushed back when he was informed that a consultant would be coming to the site to provide leadership education on Lean Six Sigma, facilitate a baseline analysis to identify critical projects, train and mentor Black Belts, and provide the site with expertise and support while executing these projects. The new CEO of this corporation had worked with our team before and knew he could get positive results in a relatively short period of time. As a result, he directed all sites within the company to engage in this process and get it done. I was selected to work with the site in France, along with sites in England and Canada. The site director in France was not given a choice. Like it or not, I was on my way.

The first day I met the site leadership team in France was interesting. We were to begin with a two-day workshop on Lean Six Sigma, which included planning the site deployment, selecting the Black Belt candidates, scheduling the training, choosing a representative value stream to use for the baseline analysis, and getting started. The energy in the room was as I expected. In fact, if I had been sitting in the audience, I might have been feeling the same way: "Who is this guy from America? What makes him think he can tell us what to do? We are already doing it. We are the top-performing site in the corporation. Just look at the numbers! We don't have time for this. We have customers to serve! We have orders to fill! We have work to do!" I am not sure how this translates into French or any other language, but caution and skepticism are not uncommon in any culture. In fact, they are necessary to some degree.

Knowing we are going to be met with the "yeah, buts," we plan on it. We build it into our model. We invite, acknowledge, and seek to understand it. Many times the reasons are perfectly valid. This shines the light back on the change agent, often reflecting changes we need to make to ensure a better connection with the people we are trying to help. It does no one any good to blame the audience or the student for a lousy performance on the part of the change agent. A masterful teacher must find ways to connect with students—especially when the students are experienced business leaders, accomplished naval officers, or well-educated rocket scientists.

In 1999, I was asked to teach some leadership and operational excellence classes for a leading defense and technology company based in the United States. This is a company with actual rocket scientists developing satellite systems, air traffic control systems, navigation systems, missiles, and advanced technologies of all kinds. Working with a team of three other consultants, our mission was to provide approximately 100 experts with integrated training on how to lead cultural transformation. The executive team for this company was looking for highly skilled change agents to pull functional groups together, improve communication and flow, and inspire more innovation and teamwork. The classes were originally designed to be three straight weeks of intensive training, with 25 participants in each class.

Within a few hours of our first class, we uncovered a plethora of "yeah, buts." Many of the participants thought they already knew it all and probably thought they should be the ones teaching the class. There were issues with control, fear, insecurity, and the need to be right. This was a competitive bunch of people, to say the least. Forcing the training on them would not work. Pushing would only be met with more resistance. This was a defense company, and the overall culture was one of dualistic thinking, fear, paranoia, and protectionism.

Day one of the training was somewhat contentious, to say the least. It was one more reminder of the ancient saying "When the student is ready, the teacher will appear." Again I contemplated the "wisdom of emptiness," or heart sutra. When we empty our bowl and let go of attachment and aversion, we can accept more of what life and divine energy offer us. A full bowl can receive no more. To be enlightened, we must drop our dualistic mindset and the heavy baggage of the past. To be awakened, we must open our mind's eye and let go of denial and competitive resistance. We must align with the Tao, the great current of life.

So what did we do? How did we deal with the "yeah, buts"? We started by looking for alternative ways to get the message across. How could we engage the class in teaching the class? These were smart people. Why not allow the students to teach one another, as well as learn from each another? Some of the participants had PhDs in science, statistics, and engineering. Others had strong backgrounds in Lean and Operational Excellence. How could we position them to share their knowledge and skills with one another, in partnership with the consultants? And because the essence of the class was on effective leadership, team-building, and cultural transformation, why not demonstrate this in class in real time and set the stage for this kind of learning going forward?

On day two, we introduced a very challenging, comprehensive simulation (game) that would require knowledge and expertise in a variety of functional disciplines to compete and win. No one in the room had all of these skills. To win, you had to work as a team. You had to share your knowledge. You had to pull people together and get aligned. You had to ask for help. You had to think interdependently, not independently. You had to apply systems thinking. We introduced and set up the competition, a simulation we designed late the night before, and let the team begin to prove their knowledge to one another. As expected, this challenge humbled more than a few people who quickly realized they had no idea how to complete the overall mission. They could certainly contribute, but they knew they needed help. The game was also designed in such a way that they would experience multiple failures without guidance from the consultants on the subject matter they knew little about.

Within 24 hours of kicking off the first of four sessions with this client, there was a shift from us-them, win-lose, right-wrong dualistic thinking to cooperative, win-win thinking. The students were now ready. The bowls could be filled. There was now context for the content. This very competitive group of intellectual people was given an opportunity to participate in the learning process in a more interactive, experiential way. Most of all, they learned that it was the "people stuff" that was most challenging. The rational problem-solving tools and statistical calculations were the easier challenges for this group. Paradoxically, the hardest stuff to learn was the soft stuff—the people stuff. They had to learn how to let go of subconscious fear, insecurity, emotional baggage, resistant thinking, and negative attitudes. They had to learn how to negotiate win-win solutions. They had to learn how to establish credibility with one another and work as a team. They had to learn how to listen with an open mind and deal with the "yeah, buts." All of the teams we set up that day to compete had the technical skills and capability to solve most of the problem. The winners would be determined mostly by their ability to develop a winning team and design a winning system.

What developed from the initial game were multiple iterations of the simulation that continued to make it more and more difficult to solve as the training progressed. With each round of the game, there was a chance for a new winning team to gain the advantage and demonstrate a deeper level of learning. The zentrepreneurs in this equation had to continue to adapt quickly to an unpredictable and changing environment. This exercise also made the training more fun. As intense as it was, the students found ways to let down their defensive guards and bond with one another—not to mention the consultants.

I used a similar approach with the site leadership team in France. Within two hours of the first day of training, the resistant attitudes started to subside. Using another simulation, the participants quickly realized that their site was making many of the same assumptions and mistakes as pointed out in the game. This awakening allowed for the seeds of knowledge to take root and the improvements to follow. Three months later, this company received a significant award for an improvement they made with a major customer. This improvement would not have been made without the learning that took place, beginning with that first executive workshop.

I now smile when I think back to a conversation I had with the site director the night before I finished the assignment. By this time we had become good friends with a high degree of respect for one another. I poked a little fun at him and asked if he remembered the resistance he and his site initially put forth. To me, it felt like I was showing up at a party without an invitation. I did not know anyone there. I did not speak the language, and I did not fully understand the culture. What is a zentrepreneur to do? He laughed and responded that he remembered and was now very grateful. We don't know what we don't know, he admitted. The sage leader recognizes this and takes responsibility for the "yeah, buts." They are merely lessons awaiting us.

A similar experience took place in 2007. This time, I was asked to facilitate a baseline analysis event for a major strategic unit within the United States Navy. We kicked off the process with one day of training on how to conduct the event and then proceeded for the next 30 days to collect the data required to complete the analysis. The "yeah, buts" started immediately: "There is no way we can conduct a proper analysis within 30 days. We need more time. We need more people. Defend. Defend. Defend." There was even a tone of hostility from a few senior nuclear engineers.

I remember clearly contemplating this challenge on a flight home from Washington, D.C. Doubt is not a welcome energy in high-performing teams, and this team was loaded with it. Resistance drains us of vital energy. How could I channel the resistant and misaligned energy of this team into focused zenergy? What was causing the resistance? Why does anyone resist? What is the root cause? Like many times before this event and many times after, I concluded that the root cause to the resistance was predominately ignorance. It is ignorance that often drives insecurity, fear, and even arrogance. We just don't know any better.

The people in this example did not understand the baseline analysis process. They had never been through one. It didn't matter that I had successfully facilitated dozens of these events around the world. They were afraid—without admitting it. They did not feel prepared. They felt out of control. No wonder they put the brakes on. It is a common human response to uncertainty. It is ignorance and fear in disguise. It comes in many forms, so the zentrepreneur must be awake and aware. We must look for it and bring it out into the open where we can deal constructively with it. What is it we do not know? What assumptions are we making? How do we know these assumptions are true? In most cases, we do not know much of anything with absolute certainty. So why do we hold particular assumptions and beliefs to be true when it is just as likely that they might not be true? Why do we believe there is not enough time? Why do we accept that we do not have the capability? Why do we resist help when help is being offered? Why do we push back when ideas and suggestions are proposed? Why do we say "yeah, but"?

I paid close attention to the assumptions and perceptions of this team and spent the next four weeks working with them to complete the baseline analysis event on time. With each "yeah, but," we opened it up for discussion and moved forward with countermeasures we could all agree on. As the team became more familiar with the process and the various data collection and analysis tools we were using, the fear subsided and the zenergy grew. Four months later, I was awarded a Naval Letter of Commendation by the admiral and board of directors for leading such an eye-opening and inspiring event. Even more meaningful to me was a comment one of the most resistant senior team members offered. On the last day of the event, he said "You know, John, you really made a believer out of me." He then went on to become one of the most enthusiastic and helpful team members in the organization.

"Yeah, buts" come in all shapes and sizes. Sometimes they come from senior management. Sometimes they come from the shop floor. Bankers use them to reject loans. Politicians use them to reject bills. Parents use them. Children use them. Team members use them. You may even use them on yourself! Listen for them. Contemplate them. Prepare for them. They are all around. Listen for the yin and the yang, the "yeah, but" and the "why not." They are two sides to the same coin. Is the glass half full or half empty? What assumptions are we making, and what can we do differently to get our point across?

One of the most memorable "yeah, but" moments for me was in 1986. At the time, I was serving as director of human resources for an automotive supplier in Michigan. This meant that I was responsible for negotiations with the labor unions at our U.S. facilities. At one facility, we sat down at the table to negotiate a new contract and quickly concluded that we were a vast distance apart. Times were tough in the 1980s for automotive companies, and this company was no different. We were losing money at the time and under great pressure from our top two customers, General Motors and Ford, to reduce prices and take on more responsibilities. In fact, these customers were demanding 25-percent price reductions during the next five years, despite increasing costs in labor, material, and engineering. We were also required to invest in Total Quality Management with extensive employee training to stay in the game.

When we shared our concerns with the labor union and supported these concerns with facts and data, including a presentation from a top procurement manager from Ford, we were simply met with "yeah, but": "Yeah, but we need more money. Yeah, but we need an increase in benefits. Yeah, but we need more time off. Yeah, but we need more security." The list went on and on. Several weeks of negotiations passed, and we made little progress. We seemed to have reached an impasse, and the lines were drawn. A strike was now looming just around the corner, and the union leadership was planning on it. What is a zentrepreneur to do?

It is wise to have a plan B. Indeed, it is wise to have a plan C. We always have options, and the more time we invest exploring our options proactively, the more creative and confident we become. Often, we discover hybrid options of A, B, and C, transcending the common either-or competitions of A versus B versus C. In this case, we explored as many options as we could, but there was no mutual agreement. The union leadership was angry and emotional, and determined to strike without sharing the brutal facts with the union membership. We were simply not in sync.

On day one of the strike, there was so much violence at the front gate that a judge imposed a court injunction limiting the union to two pickets per gate, beginning immediately. Within 24 hours, we went from a riot that made the national news to a peaceful display of disagreement. The strike ended 49 days later with an entirely new agreement in place and the foundation for a radically different culture. During that 49-day period, many employees had learned the truth about what was going on, resigned the union, and returned to work. Others waited it out in fear of retribution. The plant continued to run throughout the period with temporary help, and eventually the union leadership accepted the terms we were offering. These terms now included allowances and incentives for more cross-functional training, teamwork, and innovation. We put a new foundation in place for a new culture.

This lesson helped me immensely a few years later, in 1989, when I was asked by a client to come in and help negotiate a labor contract with their union. I saw many similar patterns and one significant "yeah, but" in particular. In this case, the company management wanted to go from six skilled trades classifications to one classification. The rationale was that this would allow the company to be more flexible and productive. This was a machine-building company, so by cross-training the skilled technicians and putting them on teams, they could manage sophisticated designs from start to finish in a much more efficient manner. The company laid out the case with clear rationale and incentives for all of the employees. There was more money to be made by the technicians for cross-training and the company would benefit from the efficiencies gained. The proposal also created more career-development opportunity and job security. It was presented as a win-win proposition. Then the union leaders said no. They wanted to keep the six classifications. These distinctions were important to the employees. Not surprising, the labor negotiators insisted on higher pay and improved benefits.

The negotiations were at impasse when I arrived, and it was clearly a "six" versus "one" challenge. The union wanted to keep the six classifications and the management wanted to go with one. I also learned that, in this case, the union was not prepared to strike and both parties were willing to agree to a short contract extension to work out a deal. This meant that management could push hard if it wanted to, without any serious risk of a strike. It also meant that we could delay a solution by extending our deadline.

I listened to both parties carefully and discovered that everyone all had very similar interests. Everyone wanted better pay and benefits for the employees, more growth opportunity and security, and more efficiency and productivity. We all wanted to improve the company's position in the market. There were just two different ways, or positions, to get there. In other words, our interests were the same but our positions were different. Maybe there is an option beyond A versus B. Maybe we can solve the problem by combining A and B, not fighting over them. Maybe the best thing to do is put A and B aside and seek consensus on option C. This is essentially what we did, concluding that the wisest thing to do is go with seven classifications. We agreed to keep the original six and support anyone who wanted to stay in the more traditional trade classification. We then agreed to add a seventh classification, Master Technician, which allowed the technicians to proceed at their own pace into a classification that combined skills and accelerated training. Within 48 hours, the contract was ratified and signed, and more than 40 percent of the workforce opted for the new classification. It was clearly a win-win, allowing people to make their own decision at their own pace. We pulled rather than pushed. We provided the environment and incentive, and then got out of the way.

I remember the president of the company was slightly perplexed by this when we first discussed it. He expected me to negotiate from six down to one, perhaps even compromising at three or four classifications. Going from six to seven classifications was moving in the wrong direction! It was outside the box! We discussed this at length, and he quickly understood that the number of classifications was not really what mattered in the long run. It was simply an assumption that this approach would lead to higher productivity. It was certainly not a fact or a given. It was also a push technique: forcing people into one classification, rather than pulling them forward at their own pace and comfort level. We know that force meets force, so using a pulling technique is much more powerful in terms of employee buy-in and commitment. Sooner or later, the company may find itself with one or two classifications if the older ones dry up, but this doesn't really matter. What matters most from a cultural perspective is that people feel enabled, empowered, and supported. I find that people can do amazing things when these characteristics are in place. Sometimes we just have to set up the game and get out of the way. The assumptions we make and the perceptions we have are often the root cause of the problem. Zentrepreneurs challenge assumptions, starting with their own.

The "yeah, buts" apply at all levels. Resistance is a common response to change. It is generally easy to spot the "yeah, buts" coming from others, but it is just as important to identify them internally as well. We all have our own "yeah, buts" to deal with. Recently, a project leader came to me with an observation and a question. Earlier in the day, he was trying to get five minutes with a production supervisor to discuss a new visual scoreboard that he was installing in the production area. He had led a team to create and install the new tool so that department personnel could see their performance day-to-day as it related to defined standards. Allegedly, the supervisor said he did not have five minutes at the time and asked if the project leader could schedule an appointment using the company's electronic calendar system. This was presented to me in a somewhat humorous way, suggesting that scheduling a five-minute appointment using the calendar was a silly, bureaucratic waste of time. On the surface, this may appear to be true, but I challenged the project leader to think a little deeper about the situation. More directly, look in the mirror and evaluate what you could do differently to have more impact on the people you come in contact with. Why did this supervisor push back? Why not give up five minutes immediately to see the new board? Why is this not viewed as a priority? Why the "yeah, but"?

Despite my prompts, the project leader still wanted to blame the supervisor for being difficult. It was a display of dualistic, win-lose, right-wrong thinking. What was missing was the realization that human beings project onto the world our own shadow, a shadow cast by our attachment to the false self or ego. We see what we look for. We attract what we are. If we are difficult to work with, we will experience difficulty when working with others. If we are negative, we will see the negative in others. If we do not trust ourselves, we will find it hard to trust others. If we blame people, we will be blamed. If we tune into the drama and crises of the daily news, we will attract this drama into our own lives. Like energy attracts like energy. In the same way, when we forgive others we are forgiven. Love others and we are loved. Be joyful and joy will come your way. We must demonstrate what it is we want in the world.

In the case of this project leader and the "yeah, but" he experienced with the supervisor, he had to find a better way to connect. I offered several questions for him to contemplate. What can you do, within your control, to help the supervisor see the visual scoreboard as more important? What can you do to improve your credibility and influence with the supervisor? Why are you not connecting? Why are you not taken more seriously?

It is easy and often tempting to blame other people for our own deficiencies. Zentrepreneurs look for solutions at a deeper level. Blame does not solve anything. If a banker turns us down for a loan, we find alternatives. We look internally at ourselves and seek the latent lessons. We look for ways to be more user-friendly and value-added. It doesn't matter if we are working with an executive team in France, a group of rocket scientists in the desert, a core of military engineers and officers in Washington, D.C., or a front line supervisor. The "yeah, but" challenge is the same. We have to take responsibility for what we can do differently, and we have to be clever in finding ways to remove the resistance. Zentrepreneurs understand that healthy living is all about flow. It is about getting into the zone, aligning with the Tao, being present and channeling the zenergy that is abundant all around us. All we really have to do is find ways to open the valves. We are often the first constraint.

I use a variety of practices and techniques to confront my own "yeah, buts" on a daily basis. To begin with, I contemplate questions such as:

- What am I attached to?

- What am I afraid of?

- What assumptions am I making?

- What thoughts am I allowing to nest in my mind?

- What are my habits, tendencies, beliefs, and mental programs?

- What good are my mental programs? What are they manifesting?

- Where am I limiting myself?

- What mental programs and viruses of the mind should I delete?

- How am I perceived by the world?

- How do I perceive myself?

- What would I do differently if I had no fear or limiting beliefs?

Questions like these challenge me to uncover paradigms and limitations I have allowed to subconsciously govern my life. They have also led me into a world of freedom, prosperity, and release that I did not know existed. By reading enlightening books, attending holistic health conferences, listening to spiritual masters, and applying these lessons to my business practice, I am finding countless ways to open the valves of zentrepreneurship even more. My greatest obstacle to moving forward with more flow has simply been me.

Here are some of the limitations I have learned to let go of:

- Self-defeating thoughts and mental viruses.

- The need for approval.

- The need for security.

- The need to be right.

- The need for control.

- The need to know it all.

- The need to figure everything out.

- The need to compete and compare.

- Feelings of fear, anxiety, and stress.

- Feelings of betrayal, jealousy, and anger.

- Feelings of pride.

- Feelings of shame, guilt, and regret.

- Feelings of grief and despair.

Each of these subconscious programs blinded me from the healing light and flow of Source energy. Rather than channeling zenergy into my life, I was resisting it—without even knowing it! My intuition was calling for attention, but my analytical mind was responding with "yeah, but." Subconsciously, I did not believe that I deserved any more than I was already getting. Thus, the Law of Attraction was delivering to me precisely what I was asking for: more of the same. To change this, I had to let go of the resistance, not fight it. I had to delete the mental viruses, not add to them. I had to empty my bowl.

One of the great challenges I have faced my entire life is the challenge of ignorance. I don't know what I don't know. And even when I do know that I don't know, I often don't know how to fix it. I know that sounds like a mouthful, but how are we supposed to fix something if we don't know how? And why would we bother learning how, if we didn't know it was broken? Demystifying this puzzle has kept me busy for many years, and I trust it will keep me busy for many years to come. This is another key characteristic of the zentrepreneur: we keep searching. We seek growth. It is what drives us and keeps us inspired. We seek ongoing improvement. It keeps us thinking positive. We are lifelong learners. When we don't know something that we want to know, we find out. We enroll in classes and we attend seminars. We read books and listen to audio recordings. We invite the wisdom and advice of great masters into our automobiles and offices by investing in the media that is available to us. We let down our mental and emotional guards, and contemplate alternative solutions without judgment. We challenge our assumptions and expose our mental viruses. One thing then inevitably leads to another, and soon we are doing things we never thought possible.

Letting go is not always an easy thing to do, especially if it requires releasing a long-time habit or attachment. Letting go of people we love is a true test of faith and character. Letting go of emotional security blankets can feel like being stripped naked and humiliated. Letting go of financial security can feel threatening. Yet if we resist letting go, we resist letting flow. A full bowl can receive no more. It is only when we rise up on the other side of the release that we realize how ignorant and insecure we were.

There are many tools available to us for releasing unhealthy thoughts, emotions, and habits. These include practices like Emotional Freedom Technique (EFT), the Quick Coherence Technique (QCT), Trauma and Release Exercises (TRE), The Work by Byron Katie, Tai Chi, Earthing, yoga, meditation, prayer, dance, exercise, art, music, writing, nutrition, fasting, detoxification, romance, laughter, and love. I actually practice all of these techniques in one form or another, and find them to be immensely helpful. You can research any one of them or all of them, as I have, and experiment with the practices that resonate most with you. True to any zentrepreneur, you have to find the practices that you enjoy most and apply them. This will be the easiest way to sustain the practice. Enjoy it! Love it. Put your heart into it. There is no one size fits all here. Find the technique that works best for you and have fun with it. In doing it you will come to know it. In knowing it, you will alter the way you see the world. You will see life in a very positive, peaceful, and inspiring way.

Checklist for Success

- I see value in resistance.

- I plan on resistance when leading change.

- I use resistance to find more balanced solutions.

- I recognize that ignorance is the root cause to most fear and resistance.

- I challenge my own assumptions first.

- I understand that blaming people does not solve anything.

- I look in the mirror first when I am met with resistance.

- I seek clever ways to remove resistance.

- I pay close attention to my audience and the perceptions they have.

- I address my own "yeah, buts" first.

- I practice a variety of letting-go techniques to empty my bowl.

- I know that when the student is ready, the teacher will appear.

8

So What!

The sage is guided by what he feels and not by what he sees.
He lets go of that and chooses this.

—Tao Te Ching

When Notre Dame expanded its football stadium in 1997, I was invited to a reception along with all former players for the university. Given the legendary tradition and culture of this wonderful school, this was an opportunity not to be missed. Players from the past 70 years would likely be present for the ceremony, including many of my former teammates. It had been 15 years since I graduated from the university, and there were a lot of guys I hadn't seen since. I was very eager to reconnect with my former teammates.

What happened next was not something I was expecting. When I arrived at the reception and began talking with some of these very talented and gifted athletes, I discovered that many of them talked as if their glory days were all behind them.

It was as if they were going through life now looking through a rear-view mirror. There was no longer a compelling vision driving them forward, no longer a big game to look forward to this week. Their great life experiences were drifting away. They were on their way downhill. I found this be quite intriguing and very memorable. These were guys I looked up to. These were guys who seemed to have it all. Some were even record-setting athletes who went on to play a few years in the NFL. Now, for whatever reason, there were no more passion and spirit in their voices. There were no more mountains to climb. There were no more dreams to pursue. The golden days were back under the golden helmet playing for the golden dome. I was stumped. I cherish and appreciate the Notre Dame experience, and I value the many lessons learned, but the past does not define me. We are defined in the eternal now, the only time there ever really is. Of course, there were many exceptions to this observation of mine, but I left wondering why some of my teammates were not taking their game and their talents to the next level—in whatever form that might be. They talked as if they were on the decline, aging and aching faster than the years required.

Appreciating and cherishing life and our past accomplishments is important. We feel good when we reflect on an award, an honor, a trophy, a medal, or a job well done. These milestones can serve as valuable reminders that we are capable of achieving success. We are capable of accomplishing goals and achieving standards of excellence. We are capable of winning. Now, so what? To rise to the next level, we have to let go of the one we are on and step up. We have to apply what we have learned to the new challenges and opportunities we face. Otherwise, we live in the past, and the future does nothing but distance us from the times we treasure most.

I remember how thankful I felt when my first book was published. This was quite an accomplishment for me, and it felt really good to feel the actual book in my hands. I flipped through the pages and read some of the passages as if it was the first time I had seen them. I wondered how many other people might read these words and benefit from them. I felt the same kind of joy when I ran through the Notre Dame tunnel for the first time. What a thrilling experience. What an amazing milestone, especially for someone who was told he could never play football again. What a proud moment. Then I remember thinking, "Let it go. Feel it. Love it. Appreciate it. Accept it. And let it go. It is now past. Empty your bowl so you can receive more."

Statistically, the number of authors who write a second book is significantly lower than the number of authors who write only one book. I remember reading this statistic when my first book came out, and it immediately got me thinking about writing a second book and then a third book. It is no wonder I now have more than 15 books published. So what if I wrote one book? So what I played football at Notre Dame? So what if I got fired? So what if I started a company? So what if I got divorced? Good, bad, ugly? So what! It is what it is. Let it go and move on.

I know this might seem harsh to some people because letting go can be difficult. Leaving a comfort zone can feel frightening and awkward, even if it is dragging you down. Habits die hard. For many people, it is easier to hang on and ride out the storm, even if we are the ones causing the storm. Quitting a dead-end job that feels secure can be frightening and tough. Why not just rationalize why you should stay in captivity and avoid the tougher decision? Why not just suck it up and dismiss your dreams? After all, they are just dreams. They are not real. Hold on tighter to the anchor that is dragging you under. Sometimes it isn't until the phoenix bursts into flames and burns to ashes that it is reborn again. Sometimes it isn't until we get fired that we see the silver lining. Sometimes it isn't until we go through a tough, painful divorce that we see the wisdom in it. Sometimes it isn't until we lose someone or something close to us that we learn a more profound truth and discover the blessings in disguise. These are the blessings the zentrepreneur seeks to find every day by letting go of pride, criticism, and judgment.

Harsh as it may seem, so what if you won a trophy in high school? So what if you earned your degree? So what if you have multiple degrees? So what if you have half the alphabet after your name? So what if you attended a great school or finished at the top in your class? Get over it. The plaques on the wall do not define you. Who wants surgery by a doctor who hasn't learned anything new in 20 years? So what if you wrote a book? So what if you wrote 15 books? What are you doing now to add value? What are you doing now to learn and contribute more? What are you doing now to give back? What are you doing now to build relationships and help people? Where are you going from here? Are you alive and thriving, or are you just getting through the day? Are you on the incline or are you on the decline? Are you growing or dying? Are you purposeful or are you without purpose? What is your passion now?

I am sometimes asked by clients to review resumes and interview candidates for certain leadership positions. For example, in December 2012, I was given a stack of resumes to review for a new position with a client, Lean Champion. This was a role I was filling on a temporary basis, and the company now realized they wanted someone in the position full-time at multiple sites. Many of the resumes looked impressive on the surface, but once the superficial trophies and accolades were set aside, most of the candidates did not respond well to the present needs and interests of this client. In fact, only about one in 10 could effectively translate past education and experience into present-day measureable solutions. It is impressive to have a degree from a credible university; it is more impressive to articulate how you use your training and skills to deliver specific, measurable results that matter. In this case, we were interested in hiring someone who could design and teach Lean classes with presence and intrigue. We were also interested in hiring someone who could effectively facilitate kaizen events and provide executive coaching and mentoring for Black Belts. During the interview, I handed the candidates a marker and asked him or her to take five minutes, unscripted, to teach me and the executive vice president a class on Lean. We also asked the candidates to describe in detail some of the kaizen events they ran and the results that were achieved. Relatively few candidates could clearly articulate the business impact of their studies and skills. In fact, only about one in 10 passed the test. The one who did was hired, and he has proven to be a very good fit. We have now repeated the same process for two other sites. The message here is that we have to stay current with the times. Lifelong learning is now the norm.

In a recent speech I gave on customer service, I pulled out an old cell phone—vintage turn-of-the-century. I then asked the audience to imagine me showing off this cell phone at a cocktail party: "Check it out. It has no wires. All you have to do is pull up the small antenna, dial a number and you can talk to people miles away." The audience laughed. They could only assume I was joking. The point I wanted them to remember is that innovations like the cell phone, as brilliant and successful as it had been, are trophies of the past. This "old" phone that I now held in my hand was being laughed at, less than a decade after it was considered to be the latest, greatest product on the market. If the company that developed it hadn't said, "So what?" the next generation of improvements being pursued by competitors would have wiped it out. Compare this old phone to the latest smartphones, and it might trigger images of the Model T from Henry Ford. Today's phones are no longer just phones. They are computers, GPS systems, cameras, video recorders, flashlights, personal assistants, calculators, alarm clocks, notepads, music players, stopwatches, and countless other devices. Before we know it, they will be chauffeuring us home in our cars. Yes, we have to cherish our victories, but if we do not learn to let go of our trophies in the past, we never elevate to the possibilities in the future. Leading a culture of innovation and fearlessness requires us to move on. There are more victories to be achieved, but it is the journey of discovery that matters most.

James Joyce wrote, "Mistakes are the portals of discovery."[1] Zentrepreneurs agree. We see mistakes as successes in disguise. If we learn something important from a mistake, how is that not a gain? This is a game-changing mindset, because it gives us a very different perspective, a very different way to look at things. The key is that we learn what we can from our mistakes and we move on. We let be and we let go. Indeed, many of the world's greatest discoveries and innovations were accidents. From penicillin to Post-Its, proactive change agents have demonstrated that fear is the real enemy. We cannot let doubt and insecurity keep us from trying something new. We have to be courageous and bold. We have to dust ourselves off when things don't go our way, and we have to contemplate why things turn out the way they do. What are the key inputs to the outputs we experience?

I remember giving a two-day workshop in Philadelphia in 1992. Five people showed up. Two were an hour late. How does a zentrepreneur respond to this? The easy thing to do might be to cancel the workshop and give people their money back. Write it off as a swing and a miss. You win some, you lose some. Another option would be to plow ahead, grinning and bearing it. Let's face it, I have to laugh now. This was embarrassing. This was a workshop on team-building and we barely had enough people for a team. If it were football, we would have been out of luck. These are the moments of truth in life, the moments that humble us and reveal a deeper sense of who we are. I decided to proceed with the workshop, guaranteeing a full refund to anyone who was not completely satisfied.

On paper, any good accountant might tell you that this workshop was a lost cause. The money it cost to market and host the event far exceeded the fees collected for five participants to attend. It wasn't even close. Now the flip side: two of the attendees were from a large company in New Jersey. They loved the workshop and asked if it was something I could provide on-site for them. The answer was yes, of course, and I went on to provide training and consulting services for this company for two years. From this perspective, the return on investment for the workshop was massive. Was the glass half empty or half full?

How often do you hear people complain? There is always something to gripe about if you look for it. People have aches and pains. People have issues with changes in the weather. People can turn sour over family disputes, work stresses, difficult people, health issues, political debates, economic challenges, and the daily drama as reported on the news. What does this mean? How does this impact our vibrational frequency and connection with Spirit? The answer is it shuts it down. When we give our attention to low-frequency energy, we fall into a trap. Misery loves company. We attract what we feel.

Zentrepreneurs approach every day with a positive and grateful attitude. We search for the value in every situation we find ourselves in, and we look for the positive characteristics in every person we meet. We laugh at our mistakes and say "so what!" to our wins and losses. Each day provides us with an opportunity to try again. We look forward to meeting new people, because life is all about relationships. There is no limit to discovering something new when we listen to people, learn their names, and hear their stories. We contemplate the problems in the world, knowing there is hidden meaning awaiting us, and pay attention to things that trouble people without becoming troubled. We use compassion to understand people who are feeling down without allowing ourselves to feel down, knowing that to help people out of misery, we cannot join it. We have to reach in from a higher frequency, a higher energetic place, and pull them out. This is true leadership. We listen to people struggling with emotional baggage and limiting beliefs, and then help them find ways to let it go. We recognize that nearly everything people cling to in life is temporary, and that because it is temporary, it evokes fear. We fear losing things and yet they are temporary. Sooner or later they will pass. The only thing that really matters is that which is not temporary. This is what we need to give our attention to. We need to attend to our soul.

Stop and consider what your soul is telling you. Do you feel utterly free? Do you wake up each day with a sense of gratitude and a smile on your face? Are you aware of the joy your spirit feels when you awaken to and appreciate the amazing journey you are on? Is your sense of adventure alive and well? Have you put your past victories and mistakes aside, and emptied your bowl for more? Do you see the abundance of opportunity all around you?

Your spirit desires to be free. It is the zentrepreneur within you, seeking adventure and expansion and expression. It is our creative and limitless Self (with a capital "S"), our connection to Source energy or God. When we put our ego and our trophies aside and we truly open ourselves up to this life-giving force, we channel a power that is beyond description. No problem seems unsolvable. There is no need to complain. There is no need to worry. There is no need to get caught up in the daily drama. There is no need to compare. We just do it. We fix the problems. We get people involved. We find solutions. We get things done.

Checklist for Success

- I appreciate what I have; I am grateful.

- I cherish my accomplishments, blessings, and gifts.

- I apply my lessons learned to the now.

- I choose not to complain.

- I see the future as bright and exciting.

- I let go of the past.

- I see mistakes as successes in disguise.

- I can laugh at myself and my shortcomings.

- I let go of things that are temporary.

- I listen to my soul, the one part of me that is eternal.

9

Now What?

Thousands of candles can be lit from a single candle,
and the life of the candle cannot be shortened.
Happiness never decreases by being shared.

—Buddha

In November 2012, my phone rang. The president of a company in Harrisburg, Pennsylvania, was on the line. He introduced himself and explained that he had tracked me down after reading my book *The How of Wow: Secrets Behind World Class Service*. He said he was interested in having me speak at his annual employee recognition event and wondered what it would take to get me there. I listened carefully and followed with a series of questions to learn more about what he had in mind and when. He then listened to me as I shared with him my availability and requirements. It was a very cordial conversation, and I appreciated his resourcefulness, passion, and interest. He knew what he wanted and he was going for it. The only problem was that he did not have enough money budgeted to cover my requirements.

Several days later, I received an e-mail from him. This time he was proposing a solution that he viewed as a win-win for both of us. If I could agree to a lower rate, he would provide me with professional videography and a local press release. He would also cover all expenses and purchase books to give to his employees. In addition, he would pitch my work to the international corporation of which he was affiliated and recommend me as a speaker for their annual event. I had to laugh. This is zentrepreneurship at its best! No wonder this man was running such a successful company. He had vision, passion, perseverance, and tenacity. In fact, I learned later that he was honored with a 2012 Top Leader award for his "wow" service by the international parent corporation. More than 400 senior leaders attended the event, and each one of them was given a copy of *The How of Wow* as a tribute to the service example he was setting. I was delighted to hear the news, especially after meeting him and speaking to his team under the terms he negotiated. It was indeed a win-win solution. The local news showed up to cover the event because of the press release he sent out and the positive relationship his company had with the media. Not surprisingly, there were many wonderful, specific examples of wow service in his organization, several of which I uncovered in my preliminary research and pointed out by name in my talk. The event was full of wows.

Zentrepreneurs understand that the world works in cycles. What goes around comes around. What we sow is what we reap. We may not always see the big picture from where we stand, but we must trust that we are part of a larger system of reciprocation.

So what is next in the mind of the zentrepreneur? What happens from here? Who will be on the phone the next time it rings? What opportunity will surface tomorrow? Who will we meet? What might we hear? With a future full of variables, how do we plan ahead? How do we know what to do next? The answers to these questions are often right in front of us, hidden only by our closed and resistant minds. They are revealed when we put forth positive thought and effort, when we reach out and take a risk. They are revealed when we pay closer attention to the people we interact with and when we witness problems in search of solutions. They are revealed when we build on ideas rather than resist them. They are revealed when we fall down and get back up again. The zentrepreneur does not worry about what is next. Worrying accomplishes nothing positive. It only attracts more to worry about. We simply look for opportunity and seize it when we find it. There is never any shortage. All this really takes is faith, commitment, and action. Of course, it doesn't hurt to prepare ourselves for the opportunities to come.

In 1988, I learned about a tool called the Myers-Briggs Type Indicator (MBTI). The MBTI is one of the most widely researched and credible personality instruments in the world. I was intrigued by it, first as a corporate manager and then as a management consultant. The tool has applications in leadership development, team-building, conflict resolution, time management, problem-solving, negotiating, career counseling, family counseling, and a host of other interpersonal challenges. How could this not be of benefit to me and many others through me? What is a zentrepreneur to do? I packed up for a couple of days and went to Ann Arbor, Michigan, to enroll in a course to get trained and qualified as an instructor. The Myers-Briggs Type Indicator is a protected tool, and it requires special training to be accessed and distributed. I completed the coursework, passed the examination, developed a workshop using it, wrote a chapter in a book on it, and then wrote an entire allegory on it, *The Eight Disciplines: An Enticing Look into Your Personality*. I cannot even begin to calculate the return on investment for that initial course in Ann Arbor. We see opportunity. We seize it. We apply what we learn and we learn from what we apply.

As I reflect back on my life as a zentrepreneur, I cannot help but smile and feel grateful for the many awakenings I have had. Many were painful at the time, but the lessons learned are priceless. Consider this short list:

- Turning a critical foot injury into a miraculous recovery.

- Turning a job loss into an exciting new career.

- Turning a company set-back into an international success.

- Turning a few book ideas into critically acclaimed publications.

- Turning the loss of a loved one into a new lifestyle.

- Turning a financial crisis into prosperity and well-being.

In 1977, I almost lost my foot in a lawn-mowing accident. This led me to a book about a man named Rocky Bleier, a four-time Super Bowl winner who was critically injured in Vietnam and was told he could never play football again. Not only did he play, but he started as a running back for one of the best teams in NFL history. This inspired me to put mind over matter and two years later, I was playing football for the same school Rocky played for, the University of Notre Dame. Twenty years later, I was given the opportunity to share the stage with Rocky at a leadership conference. My book *Reinvent Yourself: A Lesson in Personal Leadership* had just been released, and I shared my story about how Rocky inspired me at age 17 to reinvent myself and defy the odds given to me by the surgeon.

I even brought the book that my grandfather had sent me in the hospital and had Rocky sign it. The synchronicity was mind-blowing; what goes around comes around! I never planned this. It simply manifested out of positive intent and heartfelt action.

In 1988, I lost my job. My wife was pregnant with our second child at the time, and it was not an ideal time to be out of work or attempting to start a new company. The new company was set back even further when my original partners decided to bail after a few months. We had a plan, but it didn't work. What is a zentrepreneur to do? Adapt, evolve, learn, adjust, and find another way. This little company struggled, but has gone on to become an international success, providing services to some of the world's leading organizations. What is next? Who knows!

In 1992, I was encouraged to write a book. This made little sense to me at the time, because I was told years earlier that I would never make it as a writer. I took a risk and wrote *Pulling Together: The Power of Teamwork*. This self-published book continues to sell in its original form and it has since been published in three different versions by three different publishers, becoming a best-seller with two of them. In fact, *Pulling Together* spawned many other books, including the one you are reading now. Did I plan all of this? Not really. I listened to people. I paid attention and observed a need. I saw an opportunity, did my homework, and took a risk. I made something happen. And I moved on.

In 2000, I lost my father to cancer. He fought it hard and kept a positive attitude, but Western medicine could not help. This inspired me to learn more about alternative health practices, natural remedies, and preventive techniques. At a conference in California in 2011, I met a woman who shared an interesting story with me. She was diagnosed with pancreatic cancer in the year 2000, the same year my father died. After trying everything Western medicine had to offer, she was essentially sent home to die. Instead, she let go of all drugs and went to Hippocrates, a holistic health center in West Palm Beach, Florida, the city where my father died. Here, just down the road from where my father was living, she miraculously healed. Using a variety of alternative healing and release techniques, diet, meditation, and exercise, her cancer vanished. Eleven years later, she is telling me this story and inspiring me to develop *The Let Go Now Workshop.*

In the years 2008 through 2010 I was hit hard with a financial crisis. I lost all of the equity in my house and half of my retirement account, and my business took heavy losses due to the global recession. I also lost a considerable amount of money in investments that took a beating and some that went under. I went from living in a 7,600-square-foot waterfront home with boats and luxury cars, to an apartment with simple furnishings. The beauty of it all is that I have never been happier and more at peace in my life. The attachments and "things" I had accumulated over the years did not define me. They never did. The complexity of my life was a trap. Letting go of all of those attachments was my ticket to paradise. My bowl was now empty and the flow of life has opened up. Did I plan all of this? No. I simply learned to play the hand I am dealt as positively as I can.

Zentrepreneurs know how to improvise. Perhaps I learned some of this from my quarterbacking days. We develop a game plan. We orchestrate a series of plays. We plan each play carefully, detailing what every player is supposed to do. We practice the plays. And then at game time, the unexpected happens. The defense shifts. Something goes wrong. We have to adjust quickly. We have to improvise. We have to scramble. The same is true in everyday business and life: we plan, we execute, we learn, and we adjust. The real art to the game is in accepting the fact that we can't plan and control everything. We have to prepare ourselves for improvisation by learning how to transcend fear and insecurity. We have to let go to let flow.

I now see myself as a quarterback of business. The playing field is different and the rules have changed, but the leadership characteristics are the same. To be successful, we have to know how to pull people together and inspire teamwork, plan strategically, and execute the plan tactically to compete in the global marketplace. We have to keep score, make adjustments, and manage time (the clock) wisely. We must demonstrate poise and courage, take risks, and get back up when we get knocked down. We might even get blindsided from time to time, but we have to shake off our mistakes, heal from our injuries, and move on from our losses. We must be patient and present. We have to practice and be coachable. We have to accept ownership. We even have to scramble from time to time. Quarterbacking is a key leverage point in the game of football. It is a catalyst. It is a position of influence. The same is true for a zentrepreneur or any change agent in business. We have to make things happen. We have to take the ball and do something with it. In business, we use an idea instead of a ball, but the pattern is the same—though, helmets are optional!

In 2011, an idea came my way. What if I offer an event called *The Let Go Now Workshop*? What if I combine many of the release techniques I have learned over the years with my experience in fitness, nutrition, holistic health, and spiritual well-being? What if I create a workshop that aligns with and reinforces the subject matter in my book *Beyond Doubt: Four Steps to Inner Peace*? What if I bring to market an event that can help people drop their emotional, physical, mental, and social baggage and turn dis-ease into at-ease? What if?

The next question was why? Why should I do this? Why is it important? Why is it needed? Why should I invest the time and money? Why should I take the risk? These questions were answered when I did some basic research and tested the market. I started by pitching the idea to my health club. Here was an audience already interested in physical well-being, yet with a little probing, I learned that there was nothing being offered on mental and emotional well-being, and very little on nutrition and detoxification. My health club loved the idea and asked for a more detailed proposal. I worked up a plan and pitched it to them, while at the same time examining the "why not." Before I got in too deep, I wanted to assess the risk and look at it from more than one angle.

Why not offer this workshop? What could go wrong? What are the risks? What are the rewards? Will anyone show up? Will there be any liability issues? Do I really know what I am doing? I learned from this analysis that the risks were limited and the opportunity was worth pursuing. The next question was "who?" Who would I need to help me? Who would be my target audience? Who could offer and teach workshop modules that I could not? Who could I bring in to build and strengthen the team? Who could add more value to my value proposition? These questions led me to two additional health and fitness instructors who offered expertise in areas that fit in well with the vision. We now added trauma and release exercises (TRE), Tai Chi, yoga, Zumba, superfoods and detox techniques to the preliminary offering of the Ring of Peace (from the book *Beyond Doubt*), Taoist meditation and healing sounds, Earthing, emotional freedom technique (EFT), quick coherence technique (QCT), and The Work of Byron Katie—all of which I teach. We now had a more comprehensive offering of mind, body, spirit techniques.

The next question was "how?" How would we do this? How would we organize it? How would we market it? How would we enroll people? How would we handle registration and payment? How much would we charge for enrollment? How would we pay ourselves? How much time would we need to prepare? How long should the workshop be? Where should we do it and how would we secure an appropriate venue? When can we do it and why is this a good time? These questions and more resulted in a practical work plan and a very deliberate execution. The zentrepreneur knows that confusion and doubt are no friends of high-performance work teams. These questions help identify and eliminate confusion and doubt. Use them to focus and align your team for better results.

The Let Go Now Workshop was launched in January 2012 and the feedback was immediate, positive, and powerful. People with all kinds of "baggage" came and let it go. Physical, mental, and emotional ailments were addressed.

Career stress was released. Relationship challenges were dropped. People reported feeling renewed and free.

Where did this idea come from? It came from listening to several people and connecting the dots. One dot was the channeling and writing of the book *Beyond Doubt*. Another dot was my conversation with the cancer survivor in California. Another dot was my love for Zumba, a form of exercise dancing, and my passion for yoga, Tai Chi and meditation. Connect these dots with my interests in physical fitness, natural health, and superfoods, and a pattern begins to emerge. Link this pattern to my experience designing and delivering workshops around the country and my enthusiasm for teaching, and a plan begins to develop. Blend this with the physical, emotional, and financial challenges in my life—my own baggage—and meaningful motivation unfolds. In retrospect, it is almost as if I was being prepared to offer such an event. One might wonder what a serious lawn-mowing accident has in common with Notre Dame football. One might wonder what a painful divorce has in common with a spiritual book. One might wonder what a holistic health conference in California has in common with a team-building workshop in New Jersey. I didn't have to wonder long about these "dots" in my life. Connect them and a pattern emerges. These are the patterns we look for as zentrepreneurs. How do the dots connect in your life? What do you see when you observe the marketplace or the business you are in? What competencies and skills do you have, and what problems can be solved using these attributes?

Zentrepreneurs often work backward. We start with an end in mind—a meaningful vision or measurable scoreboard, for example. We begin with the market. After all, that is where the customers are and that is where the money comes from, the lifeblood of any business. What is the market looking for? What does the market want? What does the market need? Does the market even know what it needs? What is likely to be valued and rewarded in the market? How much potential is there for this value proposition? Is it worth it to pursue. What are the risks? This leads us right into the "what if" and the "why not" and the "how" questioning. What do we need to do to align with the market?

Creating a culture of innovation and fearlessness requires educating and enlightening our team with market intelligence. Who are the customers and what do they really want? Who is the competition and how do we compare? How are we performing and where are we at risk? It is dangerous to assume that our players clearly understand the interdependencies of the game we are playing, especially when the playbook, the customers, the competition, and the scoreboard remain out of sight. In competitive sports, we would think this is ludicrous, but in business it is quite common. I see it all the time.

When I was playing football at Notre Dame, we would spend hours every week going over game films. We watched and evaluated what worked and what didn't work the prior week, and we studied the competition for the upcoming week. We discussed strategy and opportunity, strengths and weaknesses. We were essentially doing SWOT analysis (strengths, weaknesses, opportunities, threats) before I even know what this tool was. We found ways to learn from our mistakes and use these lessons to make adjustments. We then took these insights onto the playing field to practice and prepare for our next event. This rigorous routine kept everyone aligned, alert, awake, and aware. We had to be focused. We had to be disciplined. To compete, we had to be united as a team.

I believe my experiences in sports have a lot to do with the body of work I do today. I remember being somewhat perplexed in my first corporate job out of school, a position in corporate finance with a large company in Chicago. When the initial orientation and training wore off, I found myself in a "corpocracy" full of wasteful, non-value-added activity. At first, I put up with it. After all, what did I know? I was fresh out of school. There had to be some reason for this work. Two years later, I experienced the same dysfunctional behavior with another company. How can the right hand not know what the left hand is doing? How can we afford to pay people good money to do duplicate or redundant work? What would the customer think of this? Can the people in the press box not see the field? Do the coaches not know what the players are doing? No wonder some of the players do not trust the coaches or the owners. There is no credibility. There is no servant leadership. There is no teamwork.

In business, there is little doubt that what gets measured gets managed. The real question, then, is, What are we measuring? What end in mind are we starting with? Do we have the right metrics? Are they aligned with optimal cash flow, regulatory compliance, and customer delight? If we do not think in terms of the overall system, we could be causing many of our own problems. The measurements we take and the brutal facts we uncover are often the best clues on where to go next. Zentrepreneurs frequently uncover opportunities by being keenly aware of the gaps between current state measures and desired state targets.

In January 2013, I helped a client in Canada complete a baseline analysis event. The purpose of this intervention was to define, measure, and analyze the current state of the business and identify key improvement projects. We trained a cross-functional team of capable subject matter experts and set to work collecting data and identifying the brutal facts. We had three weeks to gather the data, turn it into useful information, display it in a meaningful way, and prepare a briefing for senior management. The first of five briefings would be on a Monday, and the purpose of that briefing would be to get alignment and consensus on the current state. I call this the "ugly baby" day, because if the project team is not careful in how they deliver this data, it can easily be met with emotional resistance, rationalization, and even anger. Calling someone's baby ugly is not wise. It evokes a predictable, negative response that only makes things worse. The data we reveal in these baseline events is often just that: ugly! This is why we instruct the presenters to stick to undisputable facts, without criticism and judgment. Report it like an impartial, unbiased reporter or journalist, not a critic. The facts and undesirable results can speak for themselves. There will be senior managers who react as if you called their baby ugly, so be prepared. If they disagree, let them disagree with data, not opinion. This will be unlikely if we do our homework and stick to the facts.

Following the Monday briefing, we continue with daily briefings throughout the baseline event week. On Tuesday, we report on the root causes to the undesirable results, again seeking alignment and consensus. We all have to be on board the same ship. On Wednesday, we offer options and preliminary solutions that aim at each of the primary root causes, or leverage points. Given we have alignment and consensus on preliminary solutions, we move on to Thursday, where the team proposes specific projects that will solve the problems. These projects include charters that define an executive sponsor, a project leader, a project team, an overall objective, a business case, the scope, the deliverables, the timing, and the expected impact. On Friday, we have everyone sign a "Contract for Change," showing understanding, commitment, alignment, and support. This process grounds a company in the brutal facts of the current state, paints a compelling picture of a future state, promotes team alignment, and commits executive support. It often becomes a critical turning point for cultural transformation, a form of awakening.

One might ask, "How do people not know the score?" How can the executives, the managers, and the players not know what is really going on across the business? It doesn't seem logical. I agree. It may not seem logical, but it is quite common. Having facilitated dozens of these events in organizations all over the world, I frequently hear executives say, "You have to be kidding me!" when they see some of the brutal facts. Functional managers say the same thing. We understand our piece of the pie, but we never really see the overall picture. We do not have good visibility of what the customers actually experience or what the inventory turns are or what the true costs are. What may appear to be quite efficient from a departmental perspective is terribly inefficient from an overall systems perspective. For example, how can we take more than 240 days to do one day of value-added work? And how can we then sell only 0.03 percent of that product as of the 240th day? What is happening to the rest of it? Why did we have to hurry up and wait? Why did people work overtime to produce this product, only to have it sit in a warehouse? How much money do we have tied up in the material, labor, and activity related to making this product? Why are we not selling more of it faster? This is real data from this actual baseline event, and the questions keep coming. In addition to more than 200 days of finished goods inventory of another major product, why are we making more of it? Better yet, why do we have a year of supply of an expensive component for that product? And why did we just order another nine months of supply of that component? Does anyone really know the score? What is driving such behavior? Are we measuring the right thing?

In this example, the corporate procurement department is rewarded for "getting a good deal" on the price per unit purchased. With this metric, it is no wonder we might buy a "shipload" of material we do not need right away. The illusion is that we are saving money per unit, when in fact we are not accounting for the cost of increased warehousing, extra handling, retesting, expiry, and disposal. In this case, the cost of disposal of raw material and components in the past 12 months was nearly $9 million. Is this baby ugly? You can decide for yourself. Just don't tell the procurement division. Give them the numbers and go from there. Now what? How about if we start with an objective baseline analysis? There is always room for improvement. Examine your system. Examine yourself. Let the data and analysis guide you. It is an intelligent place to start.

Checklist for Success

- I know the score.

- I get the facts and analyze the data to gain intelligence.

- I look for ways to wow people.

- I understand the world works in cycles. What goes around comes around.

- I believe that worrying does no good.

- I find ways to invest in my own learning.

- I apply what I have learned.

- I turn losses into gains by finding the silver linings.

- I evaluate my performance and seek continuous improvement.

- I start with the end in mind, using a compelling vision to motivate performance.

Conclusion

We have met the enemy, and he is us.

—Walt Kelly, *Pogo*

Here is my advice to any aspiring leader, change agent, or entrepreneur. Listen to your soul. It is the one thing about you that is not temporary. It is your connection to the meaning of life. It is your conduit to Source Energy. It is your inspiration. What is it calling for? What is it telling you? Pay attention to the people and opportunities that surround you. What is being offered to you, soul to soul? Do you see it? Do you feel it? Do you recognize the opportunities in disguise? Learn to take calculated risks. Cast off fear. Apply DMAIC to solve problems rationally and free yourself from constraints. Define your current state, your vision, your dreams, your passion, your inspiration, your education, your skills, and your undesirable results. What is bothering you? What is troubling you? What are you afraid of? What keeps you up at night? What ideas do you have, and how do these ideas benefit the world in some way? Where do you see win-win opportunities? Look beyond yourself to the relationships that you need to develop in order to fully realize what you have in mind. Believe it or not, you are gifted and equipped in a mystical way to add great value to this planet, to this world we call home. You have the potential to be best in class in one form or another. The only real barrier is what you hold to be true in your own mind.

Measure your situation and the results you are currently getting. Be specific and accept the brutal facts. Let go of your defenses and rationalizations. It is what it is. You cannot change the past and you cannot change the present. The only thing you can do is influence the way you go from here. How will you respond to the brutal facts? Analyze the data. What does it tell you? What are the inputs leading to the outputs you currently experience—physically, mentally, emotionally, socially, financially, and spiritually? Find the leverage points. Find the root causes. Be prepared to discover that the most powerful root cause is you and your belief system. The thoughts and assumptions you hold to be true may not be true. Challenge them. You may be the one in the way. You may be your own worst enemy. You may be the barrier, the constraint to your own freedom and growth.

Ask what if, why, and why not to explore alternatives. Open your mind and see what comes your way. Ask who and how to build a team of trusted constituents. Surround yourself with wise and intelligent souls, directly and indirectly. Invite the wisdom of the ages into your mind through books and media to supplement your day-to-day interactions. The world is full of people ready and willing to help. Get past the idea that you have to do it all on your own, that if you want a job well done you have to do it yourself. Nothing could be further from the truth, and it is this truth that will set you free. We are not separate, competing egos. We are all connected in ways that mystify the dualistic mindset. To win, no one else has to lose. To gain, no one else has to sacrifice anything. The universe is abundant and plentiful. We simply have to learn to channel the life force in a positive direction.

Commit to continuous improvement and the pursuit of excellence. Put a smile on your face and treat people with respect. It doesn't matter if you wait tables or run a multi-national corporation. Watch how people respond when you extend positive energy. Witness the miracles that we are all a part of. Learn to be diligent and vigilant about what really matters. Apply "control" to yourself and not everyone else. Discipline yourself. Set goals. Establish deadlines. Keep score of the measures that matter. Align with the principles of zentrepreneurship and success, and watch the world unfold in front of you.

I have offered many examples from my life that illustrate how I apply zentrepreneurship to make the world a better place. Most of my experiences have been adventures and events I never planned in any detail. How could I? Life is unpredictable. Change is a given. Uncertainty is certain. We have to learn to play the cards we are dealt, and we have to learn to adjust to life's challenges without letting them destroy our dreams. We have to be prepared to scramble when the play we called doesn't work. We have to be ready to think and improvise when unexpected variables enter the equation. This is what keeps us alive. This is what keeps us on a growth curve. This is what feeds the soul.

When I finished college, I was one of five financial analysts hired to work in the corporate headquarters for the largest company in the world in its industry. I was excited about the opportunity and eager to begin my life in Chicago. Six months later, I had completed my formal training and was applying what I had learned to my job. Then things plateaued. It was as if my mind was now put on autopilot. There was no more intrigue, no more adventure. Every day seemed like the day before, a repeat performance of monotony and ennui. The pay was good and the city life in Chicago was thrilling, but my soul hungered for more. I could feel it. Something inside me called for a new adventure, a new application of my gifts.

I left my job in Chicago after two years, and started a new career in employee relations and human resources management. I felt compelled to move from analyzing numbers to synthesizing teams. During my exit interview with the company in Chicago, I suggested they not replace me for at least six months, and when they did fill the position, they fill it internally with one of the talented administrators still pursuing a degree. In other words, I was six months ahead on my work and overqualified for the position I was in. Nothing bores people more than not having enough valuable work to do. The easier thing to do may have been to stay in my job and coast, keeping my mouth shut, but I would have had to live with this. There is no escaping the truth. The life force within me called for more.

Zentrepreneurs are successful because we do not make rash decisions. Adaptable as we may be, we are also thoughtful planners. Responsibility and accountability are critical success factors for any aspiring leader. If your soul is calling for a change, apply the tools and lessons in this book to guide you on your journey. Ask the questions. Explore the answers. Think rationally and plan accordingly. Assess the risk. Identify options and countermeasures. Prepare yourself. Be discerning and diligent. Balance the intelligence of your heart with the intellect of your mind. This is how you develop good zentrepreneurial skills. You learn by doing.

When I started my new career in human resources, it required me to move from Chicago to Michigan and accept a temporary reduction in pay. The ego and intellect of the mind might not get this. It sounds backward. Yet Pascal wrote, "The heart has reasons that reason cannot know." Perhaps in the larger scheme of things, one small step backward might lead to many giant steps forward. Hmmm. Where was my faith now? Similar to my first job out of college in Chicago, I found the initial year in my new job filled with adventure and learning. I also discovered that I was much happier working with people than with numbers, even though my undergraduate degree was in finance. It was the people stuff that really motivated me.

The challenge now was the dysfunctional nature of the organization. Like many companies I have seen since, this corporation was structured in functional, departmental silos where the left hand often had no idea what the right hand was doing. To make matters worse, these functional groupings each had independent metrics driving a lot of isolated behaviors. What appeared to be functional efficiency actually resulted in cross-functional inefficiency and waste. There was also an absence of clear visibility, trust, and teamwork, resulting in the labor strike in 1986 that I mentioned earlier. Wow, what an education! The amazing thing is that, in a matter of three years, I was able to apply lessons and strategy I learned on a football field to this 67-year-old company, reinvigorating a culture of fearlessness and innovation. I use the term *reinvigorating* because I believe every company starts out with some degree of fearlessness and innovation. It has to. Entrepreneurs are known for this. We start businesses to provide value in the market, and it takes courage to do this. Someone has to step up and get it done. The problem is that much of this initial inspiration and fearlessness get lost over the years as the company matures and becomes more divided and defensive. The mission of the zentrepreneur then is to tap this original zenergy and use it to enlighten the leadership team and release the resistance. There are many examples of this referenced in this book. I was fortunate to learn it early in my career and then get a lot of practice doing it.

One of the methods I used to build trust and develop positive relationships is *gemba*. As a reminder, *gemba* is a Japanese term that essentially translates into "where the real work is done" or "where the action is." By getting away from our desks and our laptops and the many meetings that can sap our time, we go to where the real work is done and pay attention to the people who are actually adding the value to our products and services. The value-added work is what we actually get paid for—the widget we sell or the breakfast we serve. Most of this work is done on the front line by people who are often frustrated with systems that are not designed for ease of use and flow. I see it all the time. We are wise to get out and observe the work that gets us all paid. I make it a habit to learn people's names, involve them in kaizen events, and demonstrate that they are being listened to. Nothing builds trust faster than proof.

Cultures change when the systems change. Both are synonymous with "the way we do things around here." If we intend to change culture, we are wise to change the systems that govern it. This includes rethinking the work flow design, the metrics, the organizational structure, the control policies, the documentation, and all of the underlying assumptions and policies driving these systems. Our system is always perfectly designed to deliver the results we are getting. If we are getting undesirable results and we want sustainable change, we have to change the system.

In 1986, the company I was working for was acquired by a large French company. It was an asset-only purchase, which means that all of the employees lost their jobs when the deal was closed. As the director of human resources, this made for a rather interesting assignment. I was the first person hired back by the new owner, and it was my responsibility to repopulate the company. I remember thinking it was a good thing that I had gotten to know all 450 people at our main facility by name. It was also a good thing that I ended up with a new boss, a man who taught me some corporate life lessons I will never forget. In fact, it was this man, Jean Pierre Serra, who inspired me to write *Agent of Change: Leading a Cultural Revolution* six years later. Did I plan this? No, not at all, I just played the hand I was dealt.

As you continue to play the cards you are dealt in life, take time to contemplate the questions and examples in this book. Start by asking yourself if you are asking the right questions. Be curious. Awaken the pioneering spirit within you by opening your mind and exploring this mystical place we call world. The questions are relatively simple. The answers can be quite profound. Consider what comes to mind when you ask "what if?" Pay attention to how you feel when you contemplate "why" and "why not." What does it stir up inside you? What habits and subconscious beliefs does it reveal? Who comes to mind when you ask "who"? Does the "how" scare you or put you at ease? What is holding you back from exploring your dreams? Where is your current road map taking you? When you hear the question "when," do you think *now*? Do you feel a sense of urgency and excitement about pursuing your ideas? Do you feel passion and conviction? How do you handle the "yeah, buts"? Do you anticipate them and plan accordingly? Do you recognize the wisdom of contrast, of yin and yang? Do you understand the importance of harmony and balance? Do you see the context of the content?

I have found many applications of these questions throughout my career. What I find most intriguing is that life is indeed a mystery. It is an adventure. We never really know what is awaiting us around the next corner. This is what makes it an adventure. The uncertainty makes it interesting. It is not something to fear. It is an opportunity to explore and innovate, a physical playing field for our souls. It is an opportunity to grow, expand, and problem-solve. There is no end to this. It is the perfect place to learn. Scripture tells us that if we seek, we shall find. If we ask it shall be given us. Zentrepreneurs do just that. We believe in abundance and prosperity. Here is a quick guide to help you on your way:

- Keep an open mind. Contemplate your dreams. Listen to your soul. Ask "what if?"

- Play with your idea. Describe it clearly and concisely. Do not resist.

- Ask "why?" How does this idea make things better? What problems or needs does it solve?

- Ask "why not?" What is the risk of implementing the idea? What is the risk of not implementing the idea? What obstacles and constraints do you face with the idea?

- Consider what help you will need and who can help you. Think teamwork.

- Ask "how?" How do you plan to implement this idea? Who will be involved? What are the overall objectives? What are the critical success factors for this idea?

- Clarify your reasoning. What are the primary deliverables? What is the expected return on investment? How much will the idea cost, and when will investors get the money back?

- When will you execute your plan? Why is this timing right? What are the key milestones and target dates?

- Define the critical metrics for evaluating performance of the idea. How will you monitor performance and make adjustments? How will you know the idea is working?

- What "yeah, buts" do you anticipate, and how will you deal with them?

- Now, what is holding you back? Are you the one saying "yeah, but"? Are you the one in the way?

Notes

Introduction

1. The Imaginal Institute, *www.imaginalinstitute.com*.

Chapter 1

1. Diogenes Laertius, *Lives and Opinions of Eminent Philosophers*.

2. Translated by Coleman Barks with John Moyne, A.j. Arberry, and Reynold Nicholson, *The Essential Rumi* (San Fransisco: HarperCollins, 1995).

Chapter 2

1. *www.creativemovesbpo.weebly.com*.

2. *www.gembapantarei.com*.

Chapter 5

1. Ed. Jonathon Barnes, *The Complete Works of Aristotle: The Revised Oxford Translation*, (Princeton, N.J.: Princeton University Press, 1984).

Chapter 8

1. *The James Joyce Collection: Ulysses, Dubliners, A Portrait of the Artist as a Young Man, Chamber Music, Exiles* (Halcyon Classics, 2009).

Index

About the Author

John J. Murphy is a critically acclaimed and award-winning author, speaker, leadership coach, and business consultant. He is the founder of Venture Management Consultants, Inc. (*www.venturemanagementconsultants.com*), a firm specializing in creating inspiring, high-performance work cultures. John has trained thousands of people from dozens of countries and provided mentoring services to some of the world's leading organizations. He is the author of numerous books, including *Pulling Together, Sage Leadership, The How of Wow,* and the award-winning *Beyond Doubt: Four Steps to Inner Peace.* John's unique ability to draw from profound spiritual wisdom to solve modern-day problems in a practical and efficient way makes him a highly sought after teacher, speaker, consultant, facilitator, and coach.

Books by John J. Murphy

Pulling Together: The Power of Teamwork

Agent of Change: Leading a Cultural Revolution

Reinvent Yourself: A Lesson in Personal Leadership

Get a Real Life: A Lesson in Personal Empowerment

The Eight Disciplines: An Enticing Look Into Your Personality

Pulling Together: 10 Rules for High Performance Teamwork

Beyond Doubt: Four Steps to Inner Peace

Leading with Passion: 10 Essentials for Inspiring Others

Sage Leadership: Awakening the Spirit in Work

Habits Die Hard: 10 Steps for Building Successful Habits

The How of Wow: Secrets Behind World Class Service

Stepping Up: 10 Take-Aways for Advancing Your Career